Friedrich Nietzsche on Wagner

Friedrich Nietzsche on Wagner

I: The Case Of Wagner
II: Nietzsche Contra Wagner
III: Selected Aphorisms

Translated By
Anthony M. Ludovici

Printed in the United States of America and Australia.

Spastic Cat Press
www.Spastic Cat Press.com

ISBN: 978-1-61203-969-5

Contents

Translator's Preface

Nietzsche wrote the rough draft of "The Case of Wagner" in Turin, during the month of May 1888; he completed it in Sils Maria towards the end of June of the same year, and it was published in the following autumn. "Nietzsche contra Wagner" was written about the middle of December 1888; but, although it was printed and corrected before the New Year, it was not published until long afterwards owing to Nietzsche's complete breakdown in the first days of 1889

In reading these two essays we are apt to be deceived, by their virulent and forcible tone, into believing that the whole matter is a mere cover for hidden fire,—a mere blind of æsthetic discussion concealing a deep and implacable personal feud which demands and will have vengeance. In spite of all that has been said to the contrary, many people still hold this view of the two little works before us; and, as the actual facts are not accessible to everyone, and rumours are more easily believed than verified, the error of supposing that these pamphlets were dictated by personal animosity, and even by Nietzsche's envy of Wagner in his glory, seems to be a pretty common one. Another very general error is to suppose that the point at issue here is not one concerning music at all, but concerning religion. It is taken for granted that the aspirations, the particular quality, the influence, and the method of an art like music, are matters quite distinct from the values and the conditions prevailing in the culture with which it is in harmony, and that however many Christian elements may be discovered in Wagnerian texts, Nietzsche had no right to raise æsthetic objections because he happened to entertain the extraordinary view that these Christian elements had also found their way into Wagnerian music.

To both of these views there is but one reply:—they are absolutely false.

In the "Ecce Homo," Nietzsche's autobiography,—a book

which from cover to cover and line for line is sincerity itself—
we learn what Wagner actually meant to Nietzsche. On pages
41, 44, 84, 122, 129, etc, we cannot doubt that Nietzsche is
speaking from his heart,—and what does he say?—In im-
passioned tones he admits his profound indebtedness to the
great musician, his love for him, his gratitude to him,—how
Wagner was the only German who had ever been anything
to him—how his friendship with Wagner constituted the
happiest and most valuable experience of his life,—how his
breach with Wagner almost killed him. And, when we remember, too, that Wagner on his part also declared that he
was "alone" after he had lost "that man" (Nietzsche), we begin
to perceive that personal bitterness and animosity are out of
the question here. We feel we are on a higher plane, and that
we must not judge these two men as if they were a couple
of little business people who had had a suburban squabble.

Nietzsche declares ("Ecce Homo," p. 24) that he never at-
tacked persons as persons. If he used a name at all, it was
merely as a means to an end, just as one might use a magnifying glass in order to make a general, but elusive and in-
tricate fact more clear and more apparent, and if he used
the name of David Strauss, without bitterness or spite (for
he did not even know the man), when he wished to personify
Culture-Philistinism, so, in the same spirit, did he use the
name of Wagner, when he wished to personify the general
decadence of modern ideas, values, aspirations and Art.

Nietzsche's ambition, throughout his life, was to regenerate
European culture. In the first period of his relationship with
Wagner, he thought that he had found the man who was prepared to lead in this direction. For a long while he regarded
his master as the Saviour of Germany, as the innovator and
renovator who was going to arrest the decadent current of
his time and lead men to a greatness which had died with
antiquity. And so thoroughly did he understand his duties
as a disciple, so wholly was he devoted to this cause, that, in
spite of all his unquestioned gifts and the excellence of his
original achievements, he was for a long while regarded as a
mere "literary lackey" in Wagner's service, in all those circles

where the rising musician was most disliked.

Gradually, however, as the young Nietzsche developed and began to gain an independent view of life and humanity, it seemed to him extremely doubtful whether Wagner actually was pulling the same way with him. Whereas, theretofore, he had identified Wagner's ideals with his own, it now dawned upon him slowly that the regeneration of German culture, of European culture, and the transvaluation of values which would be necessary for this regeneration, really lay off the track of Wagnerism. He saw that he had endowed Wagner with a good deal that was more his own than Wagner's. In his love he had transfigured the friend, and the composer of "Parsifal" and the man of his imagination were not one. The fact was realised step by step; disappointment upon disappointment, revelation after revelation, ultimately brought it home to him, and though his best instincts at first opposed it, the revulsion of feeling at last became too strong to be scouted, and Nietzsche was plunged into the blackest despair. Had he followed his own human inclinations, he would probably have remained Wagner's friend until the end. As it was, however, he remained loyal to his cause, and this meant denouncing his former idol.

"Joyful Wisdom," "Thus Spake Zarathustra," "Beyond Good and Evil," "The Genealogy of Morals," "The Twilight of the Idols," "The Antichrist"—all these books were but so many exhortations to mankind to step aside from the general track now trodden by Europeans. And what happened? Wagner began to write some hard things about Nietzsche; the world assumed that Nietzsche and Wagner had engaged in a paltry personal quarrel in the press, and the whole importance of the real issue was buried beneath the human, all-too-human interpretations which were heaped upon it.

Nietzsche was a musician of no mean attainments. For a long while, in his youth, his superiors had been doubtful whether he should not be educated for a musical career, so great were his gifts in this art; and if his mother had not been offered a six-years' scholarship for her son at the famous school of Pforta, Nietzsche, the scholar and philologist, would probably have been an able composer. When he speaks about music, therefore, he knows what he is talking about, and when he refers to Wagner's music in particular, the simple fact of his long intimacy with Wagner during the years at Tribschen, is a sufficient guarantee of his deep knowledge of the subject. Now Nietzsche was one of the first to recognize that the principles of art are inextricably bound up with the laws of life, that an æsthetic dogma may therefore promote or depress all vital force, and that a picture, a symphony, a poem or a statue, is just as capable of being pessimistic, anarchic, Christian or revolutionary, as a philosophy or a science is. To speak of a certain class of music as being compatible with the decline of culture, therefore, was to Nietzsche a perfectly warrantable association of ideas, and that is why, throughout his philosophy, so much stress is laid upon æsthetic considerations.

But if in England and America Nietzsche's attack on Wagner's art may still seem a little incomprehensible, let it be remembered that the Continent has long known that Nietzsche was actually in the right. Every year thousands are now added to the large party abroad who have ceased from believing in the great musical revolutionary of the seventies; that he was one with the French Romanticists and rebels has long since been acknowledged a fact in select circles, both in France and Germany, and if we still have Wagner with us in England, if we still consider Nietzsche as a heretic, when he declares that "Wagner was a musician for unmusical people," it is only because we are more removed than we imagine, from all the great movements, intellectual and otherwise, which take place on the Continent.

In Wagner's music, in his doctrine, in his whole concept of art, Nietzsche saw the confirmation, the promotion—aye, even the encouragement, of that decadence and degeneration which is now rampant in Europe; and it is for this reason, although to the end of his life he still loved Wagner, the man and the friend, that we find him, on the very eve of his spiritual death, exhorting us to abjure Wagner the musician and the artist.

Anthony M. Ludovici.

Preface To The Third Edition[1]

In spite of the adverse criticism with which the above preface has met at the hands of many reviewers since the summer of last year, I cannot say that I should feel justified, even after mature consideration, in altering a single word or sentence it contains. If I felt inclined to make any changes at all, these would take the form of extensive additions, tending to confirm rather than to modify the general argument it advances; but, any omissions of which I may have been guilty in the first place, have been so fully rectified since, thanks to the publication of the English translations of Daniel Halévy's and Henri Lichtenberger's works, "The Life of Friedrich Nietzsche,"[2] and "The Gospel of Superman,"[3] respectively, that, were it not for the fact that the truth about this matter cannot be repeated too often, I should have refrained altogether from including any fresh remarks of my own in this Third Edition.

In the works just referred to (pp. 129 et seq. in Halévy's book, and pp. 78 et seq. in Lichtenberger's book), the statement I made in my preface to "Thoughts out of Season," vol. i., and which I did not think it necessary to repeat in my first preface to these pamphlets, will be found to receive the fullest confirmation.

The statement in question was to the effect that many long years before these pamphlets were even projected, Nietzsche's apparent volte-face in regard to his hero Wagner had been not only foreshadowed but actually stated in plain words, in two works written during his friendship with Wagner,— the works referred to being "The Birth of Tragedy" (1872), and "Wagner in Bayreuth" (1875) of which Houston Stuart Chamberlain declares not only that it possesses "undying classical worth" but that "a perusal of it is indispensable to all who wish to follow the question [of Wagner] to its roots."[4]

The idea that runs through the present work like a leitmotif—the idea that Wagner was at bottom more of a mime than a musician—was so far an ever present thought with Nietzsche that it is ever impossible to ascertain the period when it was first formulated.

In Nietzsche's wonderful autobiography (Ecce Homo, p. 88), in the section dealing with the early works just mentioned, we find the following passage—"In the second of the two essays [Wagner in Bayreuth] with a profound certainty of instinct, I already characterised the elementary factor in Wagner's nature as a theatrical talent which, in all his means and aspirations, draws its final conclusions." And as early as 1874, Nietzsche wrote in his diary—"Wagner is a born actor. Just as Goethe was an abortive painter, and Schiller an abortive orator, so Wagner was an abortive theatrical genius. His attitude to music is that of the actor; for he knows how to sing and speak, as it were out of different souls and from absolutely different worlds (Tristan and the Meistersinger)."

There is, however, no need to multiply examples, seeing, as I have said, that in the translations of Halévy's and Lichtenberger's books the reader will find all the independent evidence he could possibly desire, disproving the popular, and even the learned belief that, in the two pamphlets before us we have a complete, apparently unaccountable, and therefore "demented" volte-face on Nietzsche's part. Nevertheless, for fear lest some doubt should still linger in certain minds concerning this point, and with the view of adding interest to these essays, the Editor considered it advisable, in the Second Edition, to add a number of extracts from Nietzsche's diary of the year 1878 (ten years before "The Case of Wagner," and "Nietzsche contra Wagner" were written) in order to show to what extent those learned critics who complain of Nietzsche's "morbid and uncontrollable recantations and revulsions of feeling," have overlooked even the plain facts of the case when forming their all-too-hasty conclusions. These extracts will be found at the end of "Nietzsche contra Wagner." While reading them, however, it should not be forgotten that they were never intended for publication by Nietzsche himself—a fact which accounts for their unpolished and sketchy form—and that they were first published in vol. xi. of the first German Library Edition (pp. 99-129) only when he was a helpless invalid, in 1897 Since then, in 1901 and 1906 respectively, they have been reprinted, once in the large German Library Edition (vol. xi. pp. 181-202), and once in the German Pocket Edition, as an appendix to "Human-All-too-Human," Part II.

An altogether special interest now attaches to these pamphlets; for, in the first place we are at last in possession of Wagner's own account of his development, his art, his aspirations and his struggles, in the amazing self-revelation entitled My Life;[5] and secondly, we now have Ecce Homo, Nietzsche's autobiography, in which we learn for the first time from Nietzsche's own pen to what extent his history was that of a double devotion—to Wagner on the one hand, and to his own life task, the Transvaluation of all Values, on the other.

Readers interested in the Nietzsche-Wagner controversy will naturally look to these books for a final solution of all the difficulties which the problem presents. But let them not be too sanguine. From first to last this problem is not to be settled by "facts." A good deal of instinctive choice, instinctive aversion, and instinctive suspicion are necessary here. A little more suspicion, for instance, ought to be applied to Wagner's My Life, especially in England, where critics are not half suspicious enough about a continental artist's self-revelations, and are too prone, if they have suspicions at all, to apply them in the wrong place.

An example of this want of finesse in judging foreign writers is to be found in Lord Morley's work on Rousseau,—a book which ingenuously takes for granted everything that a writer like Rousseau cares to say about himself, without considering for an instant the possibility that Rousseau might have practised some hypocrisy. In regard to Wagner's life we might easily fall into the same error—that is to say, we might take seriously all he says concerning himself and his family affairs.

We should beware of this, and should not even believe Wagner when he speaks badly about himself. No one speaks badly about himself without a reason, and the question in this case is to find out the reason. Did Wagner—in the belief that genius was always immoral—wish to pose as an immoral Egotist, in order to make us believe in his genius, of which he himself was none too sure in his innermost heart? Did Wagner wish to appear "sincere" in his biography, in order to awaken in us a belief in the sincerity of his music, which he likewise doubted, but wished to impress upon the world as "true"? Or did he wish to be thought badly of in connection with things that were not true, and that consequently did not affect him, in order to lead us off the scent of true things, things he was ashamed of and which he wished the world to ignore—just like Rousseau (the similarity between the two is more than a superficial one) who barbarously pretended to have sent his children to the foundling hospital, in order not to be thought incapable of having had any children at all? In short, where is the bluff in Wagner's biography? Let us therefore be careful about it, and all the more so because Wagner himself guarantees the truth of it in the prefatory note. If we were to be credulous here, we should moreover be acting in direct opposition to Nietzsche's own counsel as given in the following aphorisms (Nos. 19 and 20, p. 89):—

"It is very difficult to trace the course of Wagner's development,—no trust must be placed in his own description of his soul's experiences. He writes party-pamphlets for his followers.

"It is extremely doubtful whether Wagner is able to bear witness about himself."

While we read:—"He [Wagner] was not proud enough to be able to suffer the truth about himself. Nobody had less pride than he. Like Victor Hugo he remained true to himself even in his biography,—he remained an actor."

However, as a famous English judge has said—"Truth will come out, even in the witness box," and, as we may add in this case, even in an autobiography. There is one statement in Wagner's My Life which sounds true to my ears at least—a statement which, in my opinion, has some importance, and to which Wagner himself seems to grant a mysterious significance. I refer to the passage on p. 93 of vol i., in which Wagner says:—"Owing to the exceptional vivacity and innate susceptibility of my nature ... I gradually became conscious of a certain power of transporting or bewildering my more indolent companions."

This seems innocent enough. When, however, it is read in conjunction with Nietzsche's trenchant criticism, particularly on pp. 14, 15, 16, 17 and 18 of this work, and also with a knowledge of Wagner's music, it becomes one of the most striking passages in Wagner's autobiography, for it records how soon he became conscious of his dominant instinct and faculty.

I know perfectly well that the Wagnerites will not be influenced by these remarks. Their gratitude to Wagner is too great for this. He has supplied the precious varnish wherewith to hide the dull ugliness of our civilization. He has given to souls despairing over the materialism of this world, to souls despairing of themselves, and longing to be rid of themselves, the indispensable hashish and morphia wherewith to deaden their inner discords. These discords are everywhere apparent nowadays. Wagner is therefore a common need, a common benefactor. As such he is bound to be worshipped and adored in spite of all egotistical and theatrical autobiographies.

Albeit, signs are not wanting—at least among his Anglo-Saxon worshippers who stand even more in need of romanticism than their continental brethren,—which show that, in order to uphold Wagner, people are now beginning to draw distinctions between the man and the artist. They dismiss the man as "human-all-too-human," but they still maintain that there are divine qualities in his music. However distasteful the task of disillusioning these psychological tyros may be, they should be informed that no such division of a man into two parts is permissible, save in Christianity (the body and the soul), but that outside purely religious spheres it is utterly unwarrantable. There can be no such strange divorce between a bloom and the plant on which it blows, and has a black woman ever been known to give birth to a white child?

Wagner, as Nietzsche tells us, "was something complete, he was a typical decadent in whom every sign of 'free will' was lacking, in whom every feature was necessary." Wagner, allow me to add, was a typical representative of the nineteenth century, which was the century of contradictory values, of opposed instincts, and of every kind of inner disharmony. The genuine, the classical artists of that period, such men as Heine, Goethe, Stendhal, and Gobineau, overcame their inner strife, and each succeeded in making a harmonious whole out of himself—not indeed without a severe struggle; for every one of them suffered from being the child of his age, i.e., a decadent. The only difference between them and the romanticists lies in the fact that they (the former) were conscious of what was wrong with them, and possessed the will and the strength to overcome their illness; whereas the romanticists chose the easier alternative—namely, that of shutting their eyes on themselves.

"I am just as much a child of my age as Wagner—i.e., I am a decadent," says Nietzsche. "The only difference is that I recognized the fact, that I struggled against it"[6]

What Wagner did was characteristic of all romanticists and contemporary artists: he drowned and overshouted his inner discord by means of exuberant pathos and wild exaltation. Far be it from me to value Wagner's music in extenso here—this is scarcely a fitting opportunity to do so;—but I think it might well be possible to show, on purely psychological grounds, how impossible it was for a man like Wagner to produce real art. For how can harmony, order, symmetry, mastery, proceed from uncontrolled discord, disorder, disintegration, and chaos? The fact that an art which springs from such a marshy soil may, like certain paludal plants, be "wonderful," "gorgeous," and "overwhelming," cannot be denied; but true art it is not. It is so just as little as Gothic architecture is,—that style which, in its efforts to escape beyond the tragic contradiction in its mediæval heart, yelled its hysterical cry heavenwards and even melted the stones of its structures into a quivering and fluid jet, in order to give adequate expression to the painful and wretched conflict then raging between the body and the soul.

That Wagner, too, was a great sufferer, there can be no doubt; not, however, a sufferer from strength, like a true artist, but from weakness—the weakness of his age, which he never overcame. It is for this reason that he should be rather pitied than judged as he is now being judged by his German and English critics, who, with thoroughly neurotic suddenness, have acknowledged their revulsion of feeling a little too harshly.

"I have carefully endeavoured not to deride, or deplore, or detest..." says Spinoza, "but to understand"; and these words ought to be our guide, not only in the case of Wagner, but in all things.

Inner discord is a terrible affliction, and nothing is so certain to produce that nervous irritability which is so trying to the patient as well as to the outer world, as this so-called spiritual disease. Nietzsche was probably quite right when he said the only real and true music that Wagner ever composed did not consist of his elaborate arias and overtures, but of ten or fifteen bars which, dispersed here and there, gave expression to the composer's profound and genuine melancholy. But this melancholy had to be overcome, and Wagner with the blood of a cabotin in his veins, resorted to the remedy that was nearest to hand—that is to say, the art of bewildering others and himself. Thus he remained ignorant about himself all his life; for there was, as Nietzsche rightly points out (p. 44), not sufficient pride in the man for him to desire to know or to suffer gladly the truth concerning his real nature. As an actor his ruling passion was vanity, but in his case it was correlated with a semi-conscious knowledge of the fact that all was not right with him and his art. It was this that caused him to suffer. His egomaniacal behaviour and his almost Rousseauesque fear and suspicion of others were only the external manifestations of his inner discrepancies. But, to repeat what I have already said, these abnormal symptoms are not in the least incompatible with Wagner's music, they are rather its very cause, the root from which it springs.

In reality, therefore, Wagner the man and Wagner the artist were undoubtedly one, and constituted a splendid romanticist. His music as well as his autobiography are proofs of his wonderful gifts in this direction. His success in his time, as in ours, is due to the craving of the modern world for actors, sorcerers, bewilderers and idealists who are able to conceal the ill-health and the weakness that prevail, and who please by intoxicating and exalting. But this being so, the world must not be disappointed to find the hero of a preceding age explode in the next. It must not be astonished to find a disparity between the hero's private life and his "elevating" art or romantic and idealistic gospel. As long as people will admire heroic attitudes more than heroism, such disillusionment is bound to be the price of their error. In a truly great man, life-theory and life-practice, if seen from a sufficiently lofty point of view, must and do always agree, in an actor, in a romanticist, in an idealist, and in a Christian, there is always a yawning chasm between the two, which, whatever well-meaning critics may do, cannot be bridged posthumously by acrobatic feats in psychologicis.

Let anyone apply this point of view to Nietzsche's life and theory. Let anyone turn his life inside out, not only as he gives it to us in his Ecce Homo, but as we find it related by all his biographers, friends and foes alike, and what will be the result? Even if we ignore his works—the blooms which blowed from time to time from his life—we absolutely cannot deny the greatness of the man's private practice, and if we fully understand and appreciate the latter, we must be singularly deficient in instinct and in flair if we do not suspect that some of this greatness is reflected in his life-task.

ANTHONY M. LUDOVICI
London, July 1911

The Case Of Wagner: A Musician's Problem

A LETTER FROM TURIN, MAY 1888
"RIDENDO DICERE SEVERUM...."

Preface

I am writing this to relieve my mind. It is not malice alone which makes me praise Bizet at the expense of Wagner in this essay. Amid a good deal of jesting I wish to make one point clear which does not admit of levity. To turn my back on Wagner was for me a piece of fate, to get to like anything else whatever afterwards was for me a triumph. Nobody, perhaps, had ever been more dangerously involved in Wagnerism, nobody had defended himself more obstinately against it, nobody had ever been so overjoyed at ridding himself of it. A long history!—Shall I give it a name?—If I were a moralist, who knows what I might not call it! Perhaps a piece of self-mastery.—But the philosopher does not like the moralist, neither does he like high-falutin' words....

What is the first and last thing that a philosopher demands of himself? To overcome his age in himself, to become "timeless." With what then does the philosopher have the greatest fight? With all that in him which makes him the child of his time. Very well then! I am just as much a child of my age as Wagner—i.e., I am a decadent. The only difference is that I recognized the fact, that I struggled against it. The philosopher in me struggled against it.

My greatest preoccupation hitherto has been the problem of decadence, and I had reasons for this. "Good and evil" form only a playful subdivision of this problem. If one has trained one's eye to detect the symptoms of decline, one also understands morality,—one understands what lies concealed beneath its holiest names and tables of values: e.g., impoverished life, the will to nonentity, great exhaustion. Morality denies life.... In order to undertake such a mission I was obliged to exercise self-discipline:—I had to side against all that was morbid in myself including Wagner, including Schopenhauer, including the whole of modern humanity.—A profound estrangement, coldness and soberness towards all that belongs to my age, all that was contemporary: and as the highest wish, Zarathustra's eye, an eye which surveys the whole phenomenon—mankind—from an enormous distance,—which looks down upon it.—For such a goal—what sacrifice would not have been worthwhile? What "self-mastery"! What "self-denial"!

The greatest event of my life took the form of a recovery. Wagner belongs only to my diseases.

Not that I wish to appear ungrateful to this disease. If in this essay I support the proposition that Wagner is harmful, I none the less wish to point out unto whom, in spite of all, he is indispensable—to the philosopher. Anyone else may perhaps be able to get on without Wagner: but the philosopher is not free to pass him by. The philosopher must be the evil conscience of his age,—but to this end he must be possessed of its best knowledge. And what better guide, or more thoroughly efficient revealer of the soul, could be found for the labyrinth of the modern spirit than Wagner? Through Wagner modernity speaks her most intimate language: it conceals neither its good nor its evil: it has thrown off all shame. And, conversely, one has almost calculated the whole of the value of modernity once one is clear concerning what is good and evil in Wagner. I can perfectly well understand a musician of to-day who says: "I hate Wagner but I can endure no other music." But I should also understand a philosopher who said, "Wagner is modernity in concentrated form." There is no help for it, we must first be Wagnerites....

1

Yesterday—would you believe it?—I heard Bizet's masterpiece for the twentieth time. Once more I attended with the same gentle reverence; once again I did not run away. This triumph over my impatience surprises me. How such a work completes one! Through it one almost becomes a "masterpiece" oneself—And, as a matter of fact, each time I heard Carmen it seemed to me that I was more of a philosopher, a better philosopher than at other times: I became so forbearing, so happy, so Indian, so settled.... To sit for five hours: the first step to holiness!—May I be allowed to say that Bizet's orchestration is the only one that I can endure now? That other orchestration which is all the rage at present—the Wagnerian—is brutal, artificial and "unsophisticated" withal, hence its appeal to all the three senses of the modern soul at once. How terribly Wagnerian orchestration affects me! I call it the Sirocco. A disagreeable sweat breaks out all over me. All my fine weather vanishes.

Bizet's music seems to me perfect. It comes forward lightly, gracefully, stylishly. It is lovable, it does not sweat. "All that is good is easy, everything divine runs with light feet": this is the first principle of my æsthetics. This music is wicked, refined, fatalistic, and withal remains popular,—it possesses the refinement of a race, not of an individual. It is rich. It is definite. It builds, organizes, completes, and in this sense it stands as a contrast to the polypus in music, to "endless melody". Have more painful, more tragic accents ever been heard on the stage before? And how are they obtained? Without grimaces! Without counterfeiting of any kind! Free from the lie of the grand style!—In short: this music assumes that the listener is intelligent even as a musician,—thereby it is the opposite of Wagner, who, apart from everything else, was in any case the most ill-mannered genius on earth (Wagner takes us as if ... , he repeats a thing so often that we become desperate,—that we ultimately believe it).

And once more: I become a better man when Bizet speaks to me. Also a better musician, a better listener. Is it in any way possible to listen better?—I even burrow behind this music with my ears. I hear its very cause. I seem to assist at its birth. I tremble before the dangers which this daring music runs, I am enraptured over those happy accidents for which even Bizet himself may not be responsible.—And, strange to say, at bottom I do not give it a thought, or am not aware how much thought I really do give it. For quite other ideas are running through my head the while.... Has anyone ever observed that music emancipates the spirit? gives wings to thought? and that the more one becomes a musician the more one is also a philosopher? The grey sky of abstraction seems thrilled by flashes of lightning; the light is strong enough to reveal all the details of things; to enable one to grapple with problems; and the world is surveyed as if from a mountain top—With this I have defined philosophical pathos—And unexpectedly answers drop into my lap, a small hailstorm of ice and wisdom, of problems solved. Where am I? Bizet makes me productive. Everything that is good makes me productive. I have gratitude for nothing else, nor have I any other touchstone for testing what is good.

2

Bizet's work also saves; Wagner is not the only "Saviour." With it one bids farewell to the damp north and to all the fog of the Wagnerian ideal. Even the action in itself delivers us from these things. From Merimée it has this logic even in passion, from him it has the direct line, inexorable necessity, but what it has above all else is that which belongs to sub-tropical zones—that dryness of atmosphere, that limpidezza of the air. Here in every respect the climate is altered. Here another kind of sensuality, another kind of sensitiveness and another kind of cheerfulness make their appeal. This music is gay, but not in a French or German way. Its gaiety is African; fate hangs over it, its happiness is short, sudden, without reprieve. I envy Bizet for having had the courage of this sensitiveness, which hitherto in the cultured music of Europe has found no means of expression,—of this southern, tawny, sunburnt sensitiveness.... What a joy the golden afternoon of its happiness is to us! When we look out, with this music in our minds, we wonder whether we have ever seen the sea so calm. And how soothing is this Moorish dancing! How, for once, even our insatiability gets sated by its lascivious melancholy!—And finally love, love trans-

lated back into Nature! Not the love of a "cultured girl!"—no
Senta-sentimentality.[7] But love as fate, as a fatality, cynical,
innocent, cruel,—and precisely in this way Nature! The love
whose means is war, whose very essence is the mortal hatred
between the sexes!—I know no case in which the tragic irony,
which constitutes the kernel of love, is expressed with such
severity, or in so terrible a formula, as in the last cry of Don
José with which the work ends:

> "Yes, it is I who have killed her,
> I—my adored Carmen!"

—Such a conception of love (the only one worthy of a philosopher) is rare: it distinguishes one work of art from among
a thousand others. For, as a rule, artists are no better than
the rest of the world, they are even worse—they misunderstand love. Even Wagner misunderstood it. They imagine
that they are selfless in it because they appear to be seeking
the advantage of another creature often to their own disad-
vantage. But in return they want to possess the other creature.... Even God is no exception to this rule, he is very far
from thinking "What does it matter to thee whether I love
thee or not?"—He becomes terrible if he is not loved in return
"L'amour—and with this principle one carries one's point
against Gods and men—est de tous les sentiments le plus
égoiste, et par conséquent, lorsqu'il est blessé, le moins gé-
néreux" (B. Constant).

3

Perhaps you are beginning to perceive how very much this
music improves me?—Il faut méditerraniser la musique. and
I have my reasons for this principle ("Beyond Good and Evil,"
pp. 216 et seq.) The return to Nature, health, good spirits,
youth, virtue!—And yet I was one of the most corrupted Wagnerites.... I was able to take Wagner seriously. Oh, this old
magician! what tricks has he not played upon us! The first
thing his art places in our hands is a magnifying glass: we
look through it, and we no longer trust our own eyes—Everything grows bigger, even Wagner grows bigger.... What a

clever rattlesnake. Throughout his life he rattled "resignation," "loyalty," and "purity" about our ears, and he retired from the corrupt world with a song of praise to chastity!— And we believed it all....

—But you will not listen to me? You prefer even the problem of Wagner to that of Bizet? But neither do I underrate it; it has its charm. The problem of salvation is even a venerable problem. Wagner pondered over nothing so deeply as over salvation: his opera is the opera of salvation. Someone always wants to be saved in his operas,—now it is a youth; anon it is a maid,—this is his problem—And how lavishly he varies his leitmotif! What rare and melancholy modulations! If it were not for Wagner, who would teach us that innocence has a preference for saving interesting sinners? (the case in "Tannhauser"). Or that even the eternal Jew gets saved and settled down when he marries? (the case in the "Flying Dutchman"). Or that corrupted old females prefer to be saved by chaste young men? (the case of Kundry). Or that young hysterics like to be saved by their doctor? (the case in "Lohengrin"). Or that beautiful girls most love to be saved by a knight who also happens to be a Wagnerite? (the case in the "Mastersingers"). Or that even married women also like to be saved by a knight? (the case of Isolde). Or that the venerable Almighty, after having compromised himself morally in all manner of ways, is at last delivered by a free spirit and an immoralist? (the case in the "Ring"). Admire, more especially this last piece of wisdom! Do you understand it? I—take good care not to understand it.... That it is possible to draw yet other lessons from the works above mentioned,— I am much more ready to prove than to dispute. That one may be driven by a Wagnerian ballet to desperation—and to virtue! (once again the case in "Tannhauser"). That not going to bed at the right time may be followed by the worst consequences (once again the case of "Lohengrin").—That one can never be too sure of the spouse one actually marries (for the third time, the case of "Lohengrin"). "Tristan and Isolde" glorifies the perfect husband who, in a certain case, can ask only one question: "But why have ye not told me this before?

Nothing could be simpler than that!" Reply:

> "That I cannot tell thee.
> And what thou askest,
> That wilt thou never learn."

"Lohengrin" contains a solemn ban upon all investigation and questioning. In this way Wagner stood for the Christian concept, "Thou must and shalt believe". It is a crime against the highest and the holiest to be scientific.... The "Flying Dutchman" preaches the sublime doctrine that woman can moor the most erratic soul, or to put it into Wagnerian terms "save" him. Here we venture to ask a question. Supposing that this were actually true, would it therefore be desirable?—What becomes of the "eternal Jew" whom a woman adores and enchains? He simply ceases from being eternal, he marries,—that is to say, he concerns us no longer.—Transferred into the realm of reality, the danger for the artist and for the genius—and these are of course the "eternal Jews"—resides in woman: adoring women are their ruin. Scarcely any one has sufficient character not to be corrupted—"saved" when he finds himself treated as a God—he then immediately condescends to woman.—Man is a coward in the face of all that is eternally feminine, and this the girls know.—In many cases of woman's love, and perhaps precisely in the most famous ones, the love is no more than a refined form of parasitism, a making one's nest in another's soul and sometimes even in another's flesh—Ah! and how constantly at the cost of the host!

We know the fate of Goethe in old-maidish moralin-corroded Germany. He was always offensive to Germans, he found honest admirers only among Jewesses. Schiller, "noble" Schiller, who cried flowery words into their ears,—he was a man after their own heart. What did they reproach Goethe with?—with the Mount of Venus, and with having composed certain Venetian epigrams. Even Klopstock preached him a moral sermon; there was a time when Herder was fond of using the word "Priapus" when he spoke of Goethe. Even "Wilhelm Meister" seemed to be only a symptom of decline, of a moral "going to the dogs". The "Menagerie of tame cattle," the worthlessness of the hero in this book, revolted Niebuhr, who finally bursts out in a plaint which Biterolf[8] might well have sung: "nothing so easily makes a painful impression as when a great mind despoils itself of its wings and strives for virtuosity in something greatly inferior, while it renounces more lofty aims." But the most indignant of all was the cultured woman—all smaller courts in Germany, every kind of "Puritanism" made the sign of the cross at the sight of Goethe, at the thought of the "unclean spirit" in Goethe.—This history was what Wagner set to music. He saves Goethe, that goes without saying; but he does so in such a clever way that he also takes the side of the cultured woman. Goethe gets saved: a prayer saves him, a cultured woman draws him out of the mire.

—As to what Goethe would have thought of Wagner?—Goethe once set himself the question, "what danger hangs over all romanticists—the fate of romanticists?"—His answer was: "To choke over the rumination of moral and religious absurdities." In short: Parsifal.... The philosopher writes thereto an epilogue: Holiness—the only remaining higher value still seen by the mob or by woman, the horizon of the ideal for all those who are naturally short-sighted. To philosophers, however, this horizon, like every other, is a mere misunderstanding, a sort of slamming of the door in the face of the real beginning of their world,—their danger, their ideal, their desideratum.... In more polite language: La philosophie ne suffit pas au grand nombre. Il lui faut la sainteté....

4

I shall once more relate the history of the "Ring". This is its proper place. It is also the history of a salvation except that in this case it is Wagner himself who is saved—Half his lifetime Wagner believed in the Revolution as only a Frenchman could have believed in it. He sought it in the runic inscriptions of myths, he thought he had found a typical revolutionary in Siegfried.—"Whence arises all the evil in this world?" Wagner asked himself. From "old contracts": he replied, as all revolutionary ideologists have done. In plain English: from customs, laws, morals, institutions, from all those things upon which the ancient world and ancient society rests. "How can one get rid of the evil in this world? How can one get rid of ancient society?" Only by declaring war against "contracts" (traditions, morality). This Siegfried does. He starts early at the game, very early—his origin itself is already a declaration of war against morality—he is the result of adultery, of incest.... Not the saga, but Wagner himself is the inventor of this radical feature, in this matter he corrected the saga.... Siegfried continues as he began: he follows only his first impulse, he flings all tradition, all respect, all fear to the winds. Whatever displeases him he strikes down. He tilts irreverently at old god-heads. His principal undertaking, however, is to emancipate woman,—"to deliver Brunnhilda."... Siegfried and Brunnhilda, the sacrament of free love, the dawn of the golden age, the twilight of the Gods of old morality—evil is got rid of.... For a long while Wagner's ship sailed happily along this course. There can be no doubt that along it Wagner sought his highest goal.—What happened? A misfortune. The ship dashed on to a reef; Wagner had run aground. The reef was Schopenhauer's philosophy; Wagner had stuck fast on a contrary view of the world. What had he set to music? Optimism? Wagner was ashamed. It was moreover an optimism for which Schopenhauer had devised an evil expression,—unscrupulous optimism. He was more than ever ashamed. He reflected for some time; his position seemed desperate.... At last a path of escape seemed gradually to open before him—what if the reef on which he had been wrecked could be interpreted as a goal, as the ulterior motive, as the actual purpose of his journey? To be wrecked here, this was also a goal:—Bene navigavi cum naufragium feci ... and he translated the "Ring" into Schopenhauerian language. Everything goes wrong, everything goes to wrack and ruin, the new world is just as bad as the old one:—Nonentity, the Indian Circe beckons ... Brunnhilda, who according to the old plan had to retire with a song in honour of free love, consoling the world with the hope of a socialistic Utopia in which "all will be well"; now gets something else to do. She must first study Schopenhauer. She must first versify the fourth book of "The World as Will and Idea." Wagner was saved.... Joking apart, this was a salvation. The service which Wagner owes to Schopenhauer is incalculable. It was the philosopher of decadence who allowed the artist of decadence to find himself.—

5

The artist of decadence. That is the word. And here I begin to be serious. I could not think of looking on approvingly while this décadent spoils our health—and music into the bargain. Is Wagner a man at all? Is he not rather a disease? Everything he touches he contaminates. He has made music sick.

A typical décadent who thinks himself necessary with his corrupted taste, who arrogates to himself a higher taste, who tries to establish his depravity as a law, as progress, as a fulfillment.

And no one guards against it. His powers of seduction attain monstrous proportions, holy incense hangs around him, the misunderstanding concerning him is called the Gospel,—and he has certainly not converted only the poor in spirit to his cause!

I should like to open the window a little:—Air! More air!—

The fact that people in Germany deceive themselves concerning Wagner does not surprise me. The reverse would surprise me. The Germans have modeled a Wagner for themselves, whom they can honour: never yet have they been psychologists; they are thankful that they misunderstand. But that people should also deceive themselves concerning Wagner in Paris! Where people are scarcely anything else than psychologists. And in Saint Petersburg! Where things are divined, which even Paris has no idea of. How intimately related must Wagner be to the entire decadence of Europe for her not to have felt that he was decadent! He belongs to it, he is its protagonist, its greatest name.... We bring honour on ourselves by elevating him to the clouds—For the mere fact that no one guards against him is in itself already a sign of deca-

dence. Instinct is weakened, what ought to be eschewed now
attracts. People actually kiss that which plunges them more
quickly into the abyss.—Is there any need for an example?
One has only to think of the régime which anæmic, or gouty,
or diabetic people prescribe for themselves. The definition of
a vegetarian: a creature who has need of a corroborating diet.
To recognize what is harmful as harmful, to be able to deny
oneself what is harmful, is a sign of youth, of vitality. That
which is harmful lures the exhausted: cabbage lures the vegetarian. Illness itself can be a stimulus to life but one must
be healthy enough for such a stimulus!—Wagner increases
exhaustion—therefore he attracts the weak and exhausted
to him. Oh, the rattlesnake joy of the old Master precisely
because he always saw "the little children" coming unto him!

I place this point of view first and foremost: Wagner's art
is diseased. The problems he sets on the stage are all concerned with hysteria; the convulsiveness of his emotions,
his over-excited sensitiveness, his taste which demands ever
sharper condimentation, his erraticness which he togged out
to look like principles, and, last but not least, his choice of
heroes and heroines, considered as physiological types (—a
hospital ward!—): the whole represents a morbid picture; of
this there can be no doubt. Wagner est une névrose. Maybe,
that nothing is better known to-day, or in any case the subject of greater study, than the Protean character of degeneration which has disguised itself here, both as an art and
as an artist. In Wagner our medical men and physiologists
have a most interesting case, or at least a very complete one.
Owing to the very fact that nothing is more modern than
this thorough morbidness, this dilatoriness and excessive irritability of the nervous machinery, Wagner is the modern
artist par excellence, the Cagliostro of modernity. All that the
world most needs to-day, is combined in the most seductive
manner in his art,—the three great stimulants of exhausted
people: brutality, artificiality and innocence (idiocy).

Wagner is a great corrupter of music. With it, he found the
means of stimulating tired nerves,—and in this way he made
music ill. In the art of spurring exhausted creatures back

into activity, and of recalling half-corpses to life, the inventiveness he shows is of no mean order. He is the master of hypnotic trickery, and he fells the strongest like bullocks. Wagner's success—his success with nerves, and therefore with women—converted the whole world of ambitious musicians into disciples of his secret art. And not only the ambitious, but also the shrewd.... Only with morbid music can money be made to-day; our big theatres live on Wagner.

6

—Once more I will venture to indulge in a little levity. Let us suppose that Wagner's success could become flesh and blood and assume a human form; that, dressed up as a good-natured musical savant, it could move among budding artists. How do you think it would then be likely to express itself?—

My friends, it would say, let us exchange a word or two in private. It is easier to compose bad music than good music. But what, if apart from this it were also more profitable, more effective, more convincing, more exalting, more secure, more Wagnerian?... Pulchrum est paucorum hominum. Bad enough in all conscience! We understand Latin, and perhaps we also understand which side our bread is buttered. Beauty has its drawbacks: we know that. Wherefore beauty then? Why not rather aim at size, at the sublime, the gigantic, that which moves the masses?—And to repeat, it is easier to be titanic than to be beautiful; we know that....

We know the masses, we know the theatre. The best of those who assemble there,—German youths, horned Siegfrieds and other Wagnerites, require the sublime, the profound, and the overwhelming. This much still lies within our power. And as for the others who assemble there,—the cultured crétins, the blasé pigmies, the eternally feminine, the gastrically happy, in short the people—they also require the sublime, the profound, the overwhelming. All these people argue in the same way. "He who overthrows us is strong; he who elevates us is godly; he who makes us wonder vaguely is profound."—Let us make up our mind then, my friends in music: we do want to overthrow them, we do want to elevate them, we do want to make them wonder vaguely. This much still lies within our powers.

In regard to the process of making them wonder: it is here that our notion of "style" finds its starting-point. Above all, no thoughts! Nothing is more compromising than a thought! But the state of mind which precedes thought, the labour of the thought still unborn, the promise of future thought, the world as it was before God created it—a recrudescence of chaos.... Chaos makes people wonder....

In the words of the master: infinity but without melody.

In the second place, with regard to the overthrowing,—this belongs at least in part, to physiology. Let us, in the first place, examine the instruments. A few of them would convince even our intestines (—they throw open doors, as Handel would say), others becharm our very marrow. The colour of the melody is all-important here, the melody itself is of no importance. Let us be precise about this point. To what other purpose should we spend our strength? Let us be characteristic in tone even to the point of foolishness! If by means of tones we allow plenty of scope for guessing, this will be put to the credit of our intellects. Let us irritate nerves, let us strike them dead: let us handle thunder and lightning,—that is what overthrows....

But what overthrows best, is passion.—We must try and be clear concerning this question of passion. Nothing is cheaper than passion! All the virtues of counterpoint may be dispensed with, there is no need to have learnt anything,—but passion is always within our reach! Beauty is difficult: let us beware of beauty!... And also of melody! However much in earnest we may otherwise be about the ideal, let us slander, my friends, let us slander,—let us slander melody! Nothing is more dangerous than a beautiful melody! Nothing is more certain to ruin taste! My friends, if people again set about loving beautiful melodies, we are lost!...

First principle: melody is immoral. Proof: "Palestrina". Application: "Parsifal." The absence of melody is in itself sanctifying....

And this is the definition of passion. Passion—or the acrobatic feats of ugliness on the tight-rope of enharmonic—My friends, let us dare to be ugly! Wagner dared it! Let us heave the mud of the most repulsive harmonies undauntedly before us. We must not even spare our hands! Only thus, shall we become natural....

And now a last word of advice. Perhaps it covers everything—Let us be idealists!—If not the cleverest, it is at least the wisest thing we can do. In order to elevate men we ourselves must be exalted. Let us wander in the clouds, let us harangue eternity, let us be careful to group great symbols all around us! Sursum! Bumbum!—there is no better advice. The "heaving breast" shall be our argument, "beautiful feelings" our advocates. Virtue still carries its point against counterpoint. "How could he who improves us, help being better than we?" man has ever thought thus. Let us therefore improve mankind!—in this way we shall become good (in this way we shall even become "classics"—Schiller became a "classic"). The straining after the base excitement of the senses, after so-called beauty, shattered the nerves of the Italians: let us remain German! Even Mozart's relation to music—Wagner spoke this word of comfort to us—was at bottom frivolous....

Never let us acknowledge that music "may be a recreation," that it may "enliven," that it may "give pleasure." Never let us give pleasure!—we shall be lost if people once again think of music hedonistically.... That belongs to the bad eighteenth century.... On the other hand, nothing would be more advisable (between ourselves) than a dose of—cant, sit venia verbo. This imparts dignity.—And let us take care to select the precise moment when it would be fitting to have black looks, to sigh openly, to sigh devoutly, to flaunt grand Christian sympathy before their eyes. "Man is corrupt who will save him? what will save him?" Do not let us reply. We must be on our guard. We must control our ambition, which would bid us found new religions. But no one must doubt that it is we who save him, that in our music alone salvation is to be found.... (See Wagner's essay, "Religion and Art.")

7

Enough! Enough! I fear that, beneath all my merry jests, you are beginning to recognize the sinister truth only too clearly—the picture of the decline of art, of the decline of the artist. The latter, which is a decline of character, might perhaps be defined provisionally in the following manner: the musician is now becoming an actor, his art is developing ever more and more into a talent for telling lies. In a certain chapter of my principal work which bears the title "Concerning the Physiology of Art,"[9] I shall have an opportunity of showing more thoroughly how this transformation of art as a whole into histrionics is just as much a sign of physiological degeneration (or more precisely a form of hysteria), as any other individual corruption, and infirmity peculiar to the art which Wagner inaugurated: for instance the restlessness of its optics, which makes it necessary to change one's attitude to it every second. They understand nothing of Wagner who see in him but a sport of nature, an arbitrary mood, a chapter of accidents. He was not the "defective," "ill-fated," "contradictory" genius that people have declared him to be. Wagner was something complete, he was a typical décadent, in whom every sign of "free will" was lacking, in whom every feature was necessary. If there is anything at all of interest in Wagner, it is the consistency with which a critical physiological condition may convert itself, step by step, conclusion after conclusion, into a method, a form of procedure, a reform of all principles, a crisis in taste.

At this point I shall only stop to consider the question of style. How is decadence in literature characterized? By the fact that in it life no longer animates the whole. Words become predominant and leap right out of the sentence to which they belong, the sentences themselves trespass beyond their bounds, and obscure the sense of the whole page, and the page in its turn gains in vigour at the cost of the whole,—the whole is no longer a whole. But this is the formula for every decadent style: there is always anarchy among the atoms, disaggregation of the will,—in moral terms: "freedom of the individual,"—extended into a political theory "equal rights for all." Life, equal vitality, all the vibration and exuberance of life, driven back into the smallest structure, and the remainder left almost lifeless. Everywhere paralysis, distress, and numbness, or hostility and chaos both striking one with ever increasing force the higher the forms of organization are into which one ascends. The whole no longer lives at all: it is composed, reckoned up, artificial, a fictitious thing.

In Wagner's case the first thing we notice is an hallucination, not of tones, but of attitudes. Only after he has the latter does he begin to seek the semiotics of tone for them. If we wish to admire him, we should observe him at work here: how he separates and distinguishes, how he arrives at small unities, and how he galvanizes them, accentuates them, and brings them into pre-eminence. But in this way he exhausts his strength the rest is worthless. How paltry, awkward, and amateurish is his manner of "developing," his attempt at combining incompatible parts. His manner in this respect reminds one of two people who even in other ways are not unlike him in style—the brothers Goncourt; one almost feels compassion for so much impotence. That Wagner disguised his inability to create organic forms, under the cloak of a principle, that he should have constructed a "dramatic style" out of what we should call the total inability to create any style whatsoever, is quite in keeping with that daring habit, which stuck to him throughout his life, of setting up a principle wherever capacity failed him. (In this respect he was very different from old Kant, who rejoiced in another form of daring, i.e.: whenever a principle failed him, he endowed man with a "capacity" which took its place...) Once more let it be said that Wagner is really only worthy of admiration and love by virtue of his inventiveness in small things, in his elaboration of details,—here one is quite justified in proclaiming him a master of the first rank, as our greatest musical miniaturist who compresses an infinity of meaning and sweetness into the smallest space. His wealth of colour, of chiaroscuro, of the mystery of a dying light, so pampers our senses that afterwards almost every other musician strikes us as being too robust. If people would believe me, they would not form the highest idea of Wagner from that which pleases them in him to-day. All that was only devised for convincing the masses, and people like ourselves recoil from it just as one would recoil from too garish a fresco. What concern have we with the irritating brutality of the overture to the "Tannhauser"? Or with the Walkyrie Circus? Whatever has become popular in Wagner's art, including that which has become so outside the theatre, is in bad taste and spoils taste. The "Tannhauser" March seems to me to savour of the Philistine; the overture to the "Flying Dutchman" is much ado about nothing; the prelude to "Lohengrin" was the first, only too insidious, only too successful example of how one can hypnotise with music (—I dislike all music which aspires to nothing higher than to convince the nerves). But apart from the Wagner who paints frescoes and practises magnetism, there is yet another Wagner who hoards small treasures: our greatest melancholic in music, full of side glances, loving speeches, and words of comfort, in which no one ever forestalled him,—the tone-master of melancholy and drowsy happiness.... A lexicon of Wagner's most intimate phrases—a host of short fragments of from five to fifteen bars each, of music which nobody knows.... Wagner had the virtue of décadents,—pity....

8

—"Very good! But how can this décadent spoil one's taste if perchance one is not a musician, if perchance one is not oneself a décadent?"—Conversely! How can one help it! Just you try it!—You know not what Wagner is: quite a great actor! Does a more profound, a more ponderous influence exist on the stage? Just look at these youthlets,—all benumbed, pale, breathless! They are Wagnerites: they know nothing about music,—and yet Wagner gets the mastery of them. Wagner's art presses with the weight of a hundred atmospheres: do but submit, there is nothing else to do.... Wagner the actor is a tyrant, his pathos flings all taste, all resistance, to the winds.

—Who else has this persuasive power in his attitudes, who

else sees attitudes so clearly before anything else! This hold-ing-of-its-breath in Wagnerian pathos, this disinclination to have done with an intense feeling, this terrifying habit of dwelling on a situation in which every instant almost chokes one.——

Was Wagner a musician at all? In any case he was some-thing else to a much greater degree—that is to say, an in-comparable histrio, the greatest mime, the most astounding theatrical genius that the Germans have ever had, our scenic artist par excellence. He belongs to some other sphere than the history of music, with whose really great and genuine figure he must not be confounded. Wagner and Beethoven—this is blasphemy—and above all it does not do justice even to Wagner.... As a musician he was no more than what he was as a man, he became a musician, he became a poet, be-cause the tyrant in him, his actor's genius, drove him to be both. Nothing is known concerning Wagner, so long as his dominating instinct has not been divined.

Wagner was not instinctively a musician. And this he proved by the way in which he abandoned all laws and rules, or, in more precise terms, all style in music, in order to make what he wanted with it, i.e., a rhetorical medium for the stage, a medium of expression, a means of accentuating an atti-tude, a vehicle of suggestion and of the psychologically pic-turesque. In this department Wagner may well stand as an inventor and an innovator of the first order—he increased the powers of speech of music to an incalculable degree—he is the Victor Hugo of music as language, provided always we allow that under certain circumstances music may be something which is not music, but speech—instrument—an-cilla dramaturgica. Wagner's music, not in the tender care of theatrical taste, which is very tolerant, is simply bad music, perhaps the worst that has ever been composed. When a musician can no longer count up to three, he becomes "dra-matic," he becomes "Wagnerian"....

Wagner almost discovered the magic which can be wrought even now by means of music which is both incoherent and elementary. His consciousness of this attains to huge pro-

portions, as does also his instinct to dispense entirely with
higher law and style. The elementary factors—sound, movement, colour, in short, the whole sensuousness of music—
suffice. Wagner never calculates as a musician with a musician's conscience, all he strains after is effect, nothing more
than effect. And he knows what he has to make an effect
upon!—In this he is as unhesitating as Schiller was, as any
theatrical man must be; he has also the latter's contempt for
the world which he brings to its knees before him. A man is
an actor when he is ahead of mankind in his possession of
this one view, that everything which has to strike people as
true, must not be true. This rule was formulated by Talma: it
contains the whole psychology of the actor, it also contains—
and this we need not doubt—all his morality. Wagner's music is never true.

—But it is supposed to be so: and thus everything is as it
should be. As long as we are young, and Wagnerites into
the bargain, we regard Wagner as rich, even as the model
of a prodigal giver, even as a great landlord in the realm of
sound. We admire him in very much the same way as young
Frenchmen admire Victor Hugo—that is to say, for his "royal
liberality." Later on we admire the one as well as the other for
the opposite reason: as masters and paragons in economy,
as prudent amphitryons. Nobody can equal them in the art
of providing a princely board with such a modest outlay.—
The Wagnerite, with his credulous stomach, is even sated
with the fare which his master conjures up before him. But
we others who, in books as in music, desire above all to find
substance, and who are scarcely satisfied with the mere rep-
resentation of a banquet, are much worse off. In plain English, Wagner does not give us enough to masticate. His rec-
itative—very little meat, more bones, and plenty of broth—I
christened "alla genovese": I had no intention of flattering the
Genoese with this remark, but rather the older recitativo, the
recitativo secco. And as to Wagnerian leitmotif, I fear I lack
the necessary culinary understanding for it. If hard pressed,
I might say that I regard it perhaps as an ideal toothpick, as
an opportunity of ridding one's self of what remains of one's

meal. Wagner's "arias" are still left over. But now I shall hold my tongue.

9

Even in his general sketch of the action, Wagner is above all an actor. The first thing that occurs to him is a scene which is certain to produce a strong effect, a real actio,[10] with a basso-relievo of attitudes; an overwhelming scene, this he now proceeds to elaborate more deeply, and out of it he draws his characters. The whole of what remains to be done follows of itself, fully in keeping with a technical economy which has no reason to be subtle. It is not Corneille's public that Wagner has to consider, it is merely the nineteenth century. Concerning the "actual requirements of the stage" Wagner would have about the same opinion as any other actor of to-day, a series of powerful scenes, each stronger than the one that preceded it,—and, in between, all kinds of clever nonsense. His first concern is to guarantee the effect of his work; he begins with the third act, he approves his work according to the quality of its final effect. Guided by this sort of understanding of the stage, there is not much danger of one's creating a drama unawares. Drama demands inexorable logic: but what did Wagner care about logic? Again I say, it was not Corneille's public that he had to consider; but merely Germans! Everybody knows the technical difficulties before which the dramatist often has to summon all his strength and frequently to sweat his blood: the difficulty of making the plot seem necessary and the unravelment as well, so that both are conceivable only in a certain way, and so that each may give the impression of freedom (the principle of the smallest expenditure of energy). Now the very last thing that Wagner does is to sweat blood over the plot; and on this and the unravelment he certainly spends the smallest possible amount of energy. Let anybody put one of Wagner's "plots" under the microscope, and I wager that he will be forced to laugh. Nothing is more enlivening than the dilemma in "Tristan," unless it be that in the "Mastersingers." Wagner is no dramatist; let nobody be deceived on this point.

All he did was to love the word "drama"—he always loved
fine words. Nevertheless, in his writings the word "drama"
is merely a misunderstanding (—and a piece of shrewdness:
Wagner always affected superiority in regard to the word "opera"—), just as the word "spirit" is a misunderstanding in
the New Testament.—He was not enough of a psychologist
for drama; he instinctively avoided a psychological plot—but
how?—by always putting idiosyncrasy in its place.... Very
modern—eh? Very Parisian! very decadent!... Incidentally,
the plots that Wagner knows how to unravel with the help
of dramatic inventions, are of quite another kind. For example, let us suppose that Wagner requires a female voice.
A whole act without a woman's voice would be impossible!
But in this particular instance not one of the heroines happens to be free. What does Wagner do? He emancipates the
oldest woman on earth, Erda. "Step up, aged grandmamma!
You have got to sing!" And Erda sings. Wagner's end has
been achieved. Thereupon he immediately dismisses the old
lady. "Why on earth did you come? Off with you! Kindly go to
sleep again!" In short, a scene full of mythological awe, before which the Wagnerite wonders all kinds of things....

—"But the substance of Wagner's texts! their mythical substance, their eternal substance"—Question: how is this substance, this eternal substance tested? The chemical analyst
replies: Translate Wagner into the real, into the modern,—
let us be even more cruel, and say into the bourgeois! And
what will then become of him?—Between ourselves, I have
tried the experiment. Nothing is more entertaining, nothing more worthy of being recommended to a picnic-party,
than to discuss Wagner dressed in a more modern garb: for
instance Parsifal, as a candidate in divinity, with a public-
school education (—the latter, quite indispensable for pure
foolishness). What surprises await one! Would you believe
it, that Wagner's heroines one and all, once they have been
divested of the heroic husks, are almost indistinguishable
from Mdme. Bovary!—just as one can conceive conversely,
of Flaubert's being well able to transform all his heroines
into Scandinavian or Carthaginian women, and then to of-

fer them to Wagner in this mythologised form as a libretto. Indeed, generally speaking, Wagner does not seem to have become interested in any other problems than those which engross the little Parisian decadents of to-day. Always five paces away from the hospital! All very modern problems, all problems which are at home in big cities! do not doubt it!... Have you noticed (it is in keeping with this association of ideas) that Wagner's heroines never have any children?— They cannot have them.... The despair with which Wagner tackled the problem of arranging in some way for Siegfried's birth, betrays how modern his feelings on this point actually were.—Siegfried "emancipated woman"—but not with any hope of offspring.—And now here is a fact which leaves us speechless: Parsifal is Lohengrin's father! However did he do it?—Ought one at this juncture to remember that "chastity works miracles"?...

Wagnerus dixit princeps in castitate auctoritas.

10

And now just a word en passant concerning Wagner's writings: they are among other things a school of shrewdness. The system of procedures of which Wagner disposes, might be applied to a hundred other cases,—he that hath ears to hear let him hear. Perhaps I may lay claim to some public acknowledgment, if I put three of the most valuable of these procedures into a precise form.

Everything that Wagner cannot do is bad.

Wagner could do much more than he does; but his strong principles prevent him.

Everything that Wagner can do, no one will ever be able to do after him, no one has ever done before him, and no one must ever do after him. Wagner is godly.

These three propositions are the quintessence of Wagner's writings;—the rest is merely—"literature".

—Not every kind of music hitherto has been in need of literature; and it were well, to try and discover the actual reason of this. Is it perhaps that Wagner's music is too difficult to understand? Or did he fear precisely the reverse—that it was too easy,—that people might not understand it with sufficient difficulty?—As a matter of fact, his whole life long, he did nothing but repeat one proposition: that his music did not mean music alone! But something more! Something immeasurably more!... "Not music alone"—no musician would speak in this way. I repeat, Wagner could not create things as a whole; he had no choice, he was obliged to create things in bits, with "motives," attitudes, formulæ, duplications, and hundreds of repetitions, he remained a rhetorician in music,—and that is why he was at bottom forced to press "this means" into the foreground. "Music can never be anything else than a means": this was his theory, but above all it was the only practice that lay open to him. No musician however thinks in this way.—Wagner was in need of literature, in order to persuade the whole world to take his music seriously, profoundly, "because it meant an infinity of things", all his life he was the commentator of the "Idea."—What does Elsa stand for? But without a doubt, Elsa is "the unconscious mind of the people" (—"when I realized this, I naturally became a thorough revolutionist"—).

Do not let us forget that, when Hegel and Schelling were misleading the minds of Germany, Wagner was still young: that he guessed, or rather fully grasped, that the only thing which Germans take seriously is—"the idea,"—that is to say, something obscure, uncertain, wonderful; that among Germans lucidity is an objection, logic a refutation. Schopenhauer rigorously pointed out the dishonesty of Hegel's and Schelling's age,—rigorously, but also unjustly, for he himself, the pessimistic old counterfeiter, was in no way more "honest" than his more famous contemporaries. But let us leave morality out of the question, Hegel is a matter of taste.... And not only of German but of European taste!... A taste which Wagner understood!—which he felt equal to! which he has immortalized!—All he did was to apply it to music—he invented a style for himself, which might mean an "infinity of things,"—he was Hegel's heir.... Music as "Idea."—

And how well Wagner was understood!—The same kind of man who used to gush over Hegel, now gushes over Wagner, in his school they even write Hegelian.[11] But he who understood Wagner best, was the German youthlet. The two words "infinity" and "meaning" were sufficient for this: at their sound the youthlet immediately began to feel exceptionally happy. Wagner did not conquer these boys with music, but with the "idea":—it is the enigmatical vagueness of his art, its game of hide-and-seek amid a hundred symbols, its polychromy in ideals, which leads and lures the lads. It is Wagner's genius for forming clouds, his sweeps and swoops through the air, his ubiquity and nullibiety—precisely the same qualities with which Hegel led and lured in his time!—Moreover in the presence of Wagner's multifariousness, plenitude and arbitrariness, they seem to themselves justified—"saved". Tremulously they listen while the great symbols in his art seem to make themselves heard from out the misty distance, with a gentle roll of thunder, and they are not at all displeased if at times it gets a little grey, gruesome and cold. Are they not one and all, like Wagner himself, on quite intimate terms with bad weather, with German weather! Wotan is their God, but Wotan is the God of bad weather.... They are right, how could these German youths—in their present condition,— miss what we others, we halcyonians, miss in Wagner? i.e.: la gaya scienza; light feet, wit, fire, grave, grand logic, stellar dancing, wanton intellectuality, the vibrating light of the South, the calm sea—perfection....

11

—I have mentioned the sphere to which Wagner belongs— certainly not to the history of music. What, however, does he mean historically?—The rise of the actor in music: a momentous event which not only leads me to think but also to fear.

In a word: "Wagner and Liszt." Never yet have the "uprightness" and "genuineness" of musicians been put to such a dangerous test. It is glaringly obvious: great success, mob success is no longer the achievement of the genuine,—in order to get it a man must be an actor!—Victor Hugo and Richard Wagner—they both prove one and the same thing: that in declining civilisations, wherever the mob is allowed

to decide, genuineness becomes superfluous, prejudicial,
unfavourable. The actor, alone, can still kindle great enthusiasm.—And thus it is his golden age which is now dawn-
ing,—his and that of all those who are in any way related to
him. With drums and fifes, Wagner marches at the head of
all artists in declamation, in display and virtuosity. He began
by convincing the conductors of orchestras, the scene-shift-
ers and stage-singers, not to forget the orchestra:—he "delivered" them from monotony.... The movement that Wagner
created has spread even to the land of knowledge: whole sci-
ences pertaining to music are rising slowly, out of centuries
of scholasticism. As an example of what I mean, let me point
more particularly to Riemann's services to rhythmics; he was
the first who called attention to the leading idea in punc-
tuation—even for music (unfortunately he did so with a bad
word; he called it "phrasing").—All these people, and I say
it with gratitude, are the best, the most respectable among
Wagner's admirers—they have a perfect right to honour Wagner. The same instinct unites them with one another; in him
they recognise their highest type, and since he has inflamed
them with his own ardour they feel themselves transformed
into power, even into great power. In this quarter, if any-
where, Wagner's influence has really been beneficent. Never
before has there been so much thinking, willing, and industry in this sphere. Wagner endowed all these artists with a
new conscience: what they now exact and obtain from themselves, they had never exacted before Wagner's time—before
then they had been too modest. Another spirit prevails on
the stage since Wagner rules there the most difficult things
are expected, blame is severe, praise very scarce,—the good
and the excellent have become the rule. Taste is no longer
necessary, nor even is a good voice. Wagner is sung only with
ruined voices: this has a more "dramatic" effect. Even talent
is out of the question. Expressiveness at all costs, which is
what the Wagnerian ideal—the ideal of decadence—demands,
is hardly compatible with talent. All that is required for this
is virtue—that is to say, training, automatism, "self-denial".
Neither taste, voices, nor gifts, Wagner's stage requires but

one thing: Germans!... The definition of a German: an obedient man with long legs.... There is a deep significance in the fact that the rise of Wagner should have coincided with the rise of the "Empire": both phenomena are a proof of one and the same thing—obedience and long legs.—Never have people been more obedient, never have they been so well ordered about. The conductors of Wagnerian orchestras, more particularly, are worthy of an age, which posterity will one day call, with timid awe, the classical age of war.

Wagner understood how to command; in this respect, too, he was a great teacher. He commanded as a man who had exercised an inexorable will over himself—as one who had practised lifelong discipline: Wagner was, perhaps, the greatest example of self-violence in the whole of the history of art (—even Alfieri, who in other respects is his next-of-kin, is outdone by him. The note of a Torinese).

12

This view, that our actors have become more worthy of respect than heretofore, does not imply that I believe them to have become less dangerous.... But who is in any doubt as to what I want,—as to what the three requisitions are concerning which my wrath and my care and love of art, have made me open my mouth on this occasion?

That the stage should not become master of the arts.

That the actor should not become the corrupter of the genuine.

That music should not become an art of lying.

Friedrich Nietzsche.

Postscript

The gravity of these last words allows me at this point to introduce a few sentences out of an unprinted essay which will at least leave no doubt as to my earnestness in regard to this question. The title of this essay is: "What Wagner has cost us."

One pays dearly for having been a follower of Wagner. Even

to-day a vague feeling that this is so, still prevails. Even Wagner's success, his triumph, did not uproot this feeling thoroughly. But formerly it was strong, it was terrible, it was a
gloomy hate throughout almost three-quarters of Wagner's
life. The resistance which he met with among us Germans
cannot be too highly valued or too highly honoured. People
guarded themselves against him as against an illness,—not
with arguments—it is impossible to refute an illness,—but
with obstruction, with mistrust, with repugnance, with loathing, with somber earnestness, as though he were a great rampant danger. The æsthetes gave themselves away when out
of three schools of German philosophy they waged an absurd
war against Wagner's principles with "ifs" and "fors"—what
did he care about principles, even his own!—The Germans
themselves had enough instinctive good sense to dispense
with every "if" and "for" in this matter. An instinct is weakened when it becomes conscious: for by becoming conscious
it makes itself feeble. If there were any signs that in spite of
the universal character of European decadence there was still
a modicum of health, still an instinctive premonition of what
is harmful and dangerous, residing in the German soul, then
it would be precisely this blunt resistance to Wagner which
I should least like to see underrated. It does us honour, it
gives us some reason to hope: France no longer has such an
amount of health at her disposal. The Germans, these loi-
terers par excellence, as history shows, are to-day the most
backward among the civilized nations of Europe; this has its
advantages,—for they are thus relatively the youngest.

One pays dearly for having been a follower of Wagner. It is
only quite recently that the Germans have overcome a sort of
dread of him,—the desire to be rid of him occurred to them
again and again.[12] Does anybody remember a very curious
occurrence in which, quite unexpectedly towards the end,
this old feeling once more manifested itself? It happened at
Wagner's funeral. The first Wagner Society, the one in Mu-
nich, laid a wreath on his grave with this inscription, which
immediately became famous: "Salvation to the Saviour!" Everybody admired the lofty inspiration which had dictated this

inscription, as also the taste which seemed to be the privilege of the followers of Wagner. Many also, however (it was singular enough), made this slight alteration in it: "Salvation from the Saviour"—People began to breathe again—

One pays dearly for having been a follower of Wagner. Let us try to estimate the influence of this worship upon culture. Whom did this movement press to the front? What did it make ever more and more pre-eminent?—In the first place the layman's arrogance, the arrogance of the art-maniac. Now these people are organizing societies, they wish to make their taste prevail, they even wish to pose as judges in rebus musicis et musicantibus. Secondly: an ever increasing indifference towards severe, noble and conscientious schooling in the service of art, and in its place the belief in genius, or in plain English, cheeky dilettantism (—the formula for this is to be found in the Mastersingers). Thirdly, and this is the worst of all: Theatrocracy—, the craziness of a belief in the pre-eminence of the theatre, in the right of the theatre to rule supreme over the arts, over Art in general.... But this should be shouted into the face of Wagnerites a hundred times over: that the theatre is something lower than art, something secondary, something coarsened, above all something suitably distorted and falsified for the mob. In this respect Wagner altered nothing: Bayreuth is grand Opera—and not even good opera.... The stage is a form of Demolatry in the realm of taste, the stage is an insurrection of the mob, a plébiscite against good taste.... The case of Wagner proves this fact: he captivated the masses—he depraved taste, he even perverted our taste for opera!—

One pays dearly for having been a follower of Wagner. What has Wagner-worship made out of spirit? Does Wagner liberate the spirit? To him belong that ambiguity and equivocation and all other qualities which can convince the uncertain without making them conscious of why they have been convinced. In this sense Wagner is a seducer on a grand scale. There is nothing exhausted, nothing effete, nothing dangerous to life, nothing that slanders the world in the realm of spirit, which has not secretly found shelter in his art, he

conceals the blackest obscurantism in the luminous orbs of
the ideal. He flatters every nihilistic (Buddhistic) instinct and
togs it out in music; he flatters every form of Christianity,
every religious expression of decadence. He that hath ears to
hear let him hear: everything that has ever grown out of the
soil of impoverished life, the whole counterfeit coinage of the
transcendental and of a Beyond found its most sublime ad-
vocate in Wagner's art, not in formulæ (Wagner is too clever
to use formulæ), but in the persuasion of the senses which
in their turn makes the spirit weary and morbid. Music in
the form of Circe ... in this respect his last work is his greatest masterpiece. In the art of seduction "Parsifal" will forever
maintain its rank as a stroke of genius.... I admire this work.
I would fain have composed it myself. Wagner was never better inspired than towards the end. The subtlety with which
beauty and disease are united here, reaches such a height,
that it casts so to speak a shadow upon all Wagner's earlier
achievements: it seems too bright, too healthy. Do ye understand this? Health and brightness acting like a shadow? Almost like an objection?... To this extent are we already pure
fools.... Never was there a greater Master in heavy hieratic
perfumes—Never on earth has there been such a connoisseur
of paltry infinities, of all that thrills, of extravagant excesses,
of all the feminism from out the vocabulary of happiness! My
friends, do but drink the philtres of this art! Nowhere will
ye find a more pleasant method of enervating your spirit, of
forgetting your manliness in the shade of a rosebush.... Ah,
this old magician, mightiest of Klingsors; how he wages war
against us with his art, against us free spirits! How he appeals to every form of cowardice of the modern soul with his
charming girlish notes! There never was such a mortal hatred of knowledge! One must be a very cynic in order to resist
seduction here. One must be able to bite in order to resist
worshipping at this shrine. Very well, old seducer! The cynic
cautions you—cave canem....

One pays dearly for having been a follower of Wagner. I
contemplate the youthlets who have long been exposed to
his infection. The first relatively innocuous effect of it is the

corruption of their taste. Wagner acts like chronic recourse to the bottle. He stultifies, he befouls the stomach. His specific effect: degeneration of the feeling for rhythm. What the Wagnerite calls rhythmical is what I call, to use a Greek metaphor, "stirring a swamp." Much more dangerous than all this, however, is the corruption of ideas. The youthlet becomes a moon-calf, an "idealist". He stands above science, and in this respect he has reached the master's heights. On the other hand, he assumes the airs of a philosopher, he writes for the Bayreuth Journal; he solves all problems in the name of the Father, the Son, and the Holy Master. But the most ghastly thing of all is the deterioration of the nerves. Let anyone wander through a large city at night, in all directions he will hear people doing violence to instruments with solemn rage and fury, a wild uproar breaks out at intervals. What is happening? It is the disciples of Wagner in the act of worshipping him.... Bayreuth is another word for a Hydro. A typical telegram from Bayreuth would read bereits bereut (I already repent). Wagner is bad for young men; he is fatal for women. What medically speaking is a female Wagnerite? It seems to me that a doctor could not be too serious in putting this alternative of conscience to young women; either one thing or the other. But they have already made their choice. You cannot serve two Masters when one of these is Wagner. Wagner redeemed woman; and in return woman built Bayreuth for him. Every sacrifice, every surrender: there was nothing that they were not prepared to give him. Woman impoverishes herself in favour of the Master, she becomes quite touching, she stands naked before him. The female Wagnerite, the most attractive equivocality that exists to-day: she is the incarnation of Wagner's cause: his cause triumphs with her as its symbol.... Ah, this old robber! He robs our young men: he even robs our women as well, and drags them to his cell.... Ah, this old Minotaur! What has he not already cost us? Every year processions of the finest young men and maidens are led into his labyrinth that he may swallow them up, every year the whole of Europe cries out "Away to Crete! Away to Crete!"....

Second Postscript

It seems to me that my letter is open to some misunderstanding. On certain faces I see the expression of gratitude; I even hear modest but merry laughter. I prefer to be understood here as in other things. But since a certain animal, the worm of Empire, the famous Rhinoxera, has become lodged in the vineyards of the German spirit, nobody any longer understands a word I say. The Kreus-Zeitung has brought this home to me, not to speak of the Litterarisches Centralblatt. I have given the Germans the deepest books that they have ever possessed—a sufficient reason for their not having understood a word of them.... If in this essay I declare war against Wagner—and incidentally against a certain form of German taste, if I seem to use strong language about the cretinism of Bayreuth, it must not be supposed that I am in the least anxious to glorify any other musician. Other musicians are not to be considered by the side of Wagner. Things are generally bad. Decay is universal. Disease lies at the very root of things. If Wagner's name represents the ruin of music, just as Bernini's stands for the ruin of sculpture, he is not on that account its cause. All he did was to accelerate the fall,—though we are quite prepared to admit that he did it in a way which makes one recoil with horror from this almost instantaneous decline and fall to the depths. He possessed the ingenuousness of decadence: this constituted his superiority. He believed in it. He did not halt before any of its logical consequences. The others hesitated—that is their distinction. They have no other. What is common to both Wagner and "the others" consists in this: the decline of all organizing power, the abuse of traditional means, without the capacity or the aim that would justify this. The counterfeit imitation of grand forms, for which nobody nowadays is strong, proud, self-reliant and healthy enough, excessive vitality in small details; passion at all costs; refinement as an expression of impoverished life, ever more nerves in the place of muscle. I know only one musician who to-day would be able to compose an overture as an organic whole: and nobody else knows him.[13] He who is famous now, does not write better music than Wagner, but only less characteristic, less definite music:—less definite, because half measures, even in decadence, cannot stand by the side of completeness. But Wagner was complete, Wagner represented thorough corruption, Wagner has had the courage, the will, and the conviction for corruption. What does Johannes Brahms matter?... It was his good fortune to be misunderstood by Germany; he was taken to be an antagonist of Wagner—people required an antagonist!—But he did not write necessary music, above all he wrote too much music!—When one is not rich one should at least have enough pride to be poor!... The sympathy which here and there was meted out to Brahms, apart from party interests and party misunderstandings, was for a long time a riddle to me, until one day through an accident, almost, I discovered that he affected a particular type of man. He has the melancholy of impotence. His creations are not the result of plenitude, he thirsts after abundance. Apart from what he plagiarizes, from what he borrows from ancient or exotically modern styles—he is a master in the art of copying,—there remains as his most individual quality a longing.... And this is what the dissatisfied of all kinds, and all those who yearn, divine in him. He is much too little of a personality, too little of a central figure.... The "impersonal," those who are not self-centered, love him for this. He is especially the musician of a species of dissatisfied women. Fifty steps further on, and we find the female Wagnerite—just as we find Wagner himself fifty paces ahead of Brahms.—The female Wagnerite is a more definite, a more interesting, and above all, a more attractive type. Brahms is touching so long as he dreams or mourns over himself in private—in this respect he is modern;—he becomes cold, we no longer feel at one with him when he poses as the child of the classics.... People like to call Brahms Beethoven's heir: I know of no more cautious euphemism—All that which to-day makes a claim to being the grand style in music is on precisely that account either false to us or false to itself. This alternative is suspicious enough: in itself it contains a casuistic question concerning the value of the two cases. The instinct of the majority pro-

tests against the alternative; "false to us"—they do not wish
to be cheated;—and I myself would certainly always prefer
this type to the other ("False to itself"). This is my taste.—
Expressed more clearly for the sake of the "poor in spirit"
it amounts to this: Brahms or Wagner.... Brahms is not an
actor.—A very great part of other musicians may be summed
up in the concept Brahms—I do not wish to say anything
about the clever apes of Wagner, as for instance Goldmark:
when one has "The Queen of Sheba" to one's name, one belongs to a menagerie,—one ought to put oneself on show.—
Nowadays all things that can be done well and even with a
master hand are small. In this department alone is honesty
still possible. Nothing, however, can cure music as a whole
of its chief fault, of its fate, which is to be the expression of
general physiological contradiction,—which is, in fact, to be
modern.

The best instruction, the most conscientious schooling,
the most thorough familiarity, yea, and even isolation, with
the Old Masters,—all this only acts as a palliative, or, more
strictly speaking, has but an illusory effect, because the first
condition of the right thing is no longer in our bodies; whether this first condition be the strong race of a Handel or the
overflowing animal spirits of a Rossini. Not everyone has the
right to every teacher: and this holds good of whole epochs.—
In itself it is not impossible that there are still remains of
stronger natures, typical unadapted men, somewhere in Europe: from this quarter the advent of a somewhat belated
form of beauty and perfection, even in music, might still be
hoped for. But the most that we can expect to see are exceptional cases. From the rule, that corruption is paramount,
that corruption is a fatality,—not even a God can save music.

Epilogue

And now let us take breath and withdraw a moment from
this narrow world which necessarily must be narrow, because we have to make enquiries relative to the value of persons. A philosopher feels that he wants to wash his hands
after he has concerned himself so long with the "Case of

Wagner". I shall now give my notion of what is modern. According to the measure of energy of every age, there is also a
standard that determines which virtues shall be allowed and
which forbidden. The age either has the virtues of ascending
life, in which case it resists the virtues of degeneration with
all its deepest instincts. Or it is in itself an age of degeneration, in which case it requires the virtues of declining life,—
in which case it hates everything that justifies itself, solely
as being the outcome of a plenitude, or a superabundance
of strength. Æsthetic is inextricably bound up with these
biological principles: there is decadent æsthetic, and classical æsthetic,—"beauty in itself" is just as much a chimera as
any other kind of idealism.—Within the narrow sphere of the
so-called moral values, no greater antithesis could be found
than that of master-morality and the morality of Christian
valuations: the latter having grown out of a thoroughly morbid soil. (—The gospels present us with the same physiological types, as do the novels of Dostoiewsky), the master-
morality ("Roman," "pagan," "classical," "Renaissance"), on
the other hand, being the symbolic speech of well-constitut-
edness, of ascending life, and of the Will to Power as a vital principle. Master-morality affirms just as instinctively as
Christian morality denies ("God," "Beyond," "self-denial,"—
all of them negations). The first reflects its plenitude upon
things,—it transfigures, it embellishes, it rationalizes the
world,—the latter impoverishes, bleaches, mars the value of
things; it suppresses the world. "World" is a Christian term
of abuse. These antithetical forms in the optics of values,
are both necessary: they are different points of view which
cannot be circumvented either with arguments or counter-
arguments. One cannot refute Christianity: it is impossible
to refute a diseased eyesight. That people should have com-
bated pessimism as if it had been a philosophy, was the very
acme of learned stupidity. The concepts "true" and "untrue"
do not seem to me to have any sense in optics.—That, alone,
which has to be guarded against is the falsity, the instinctive
duplicity which would fain regard this antithesis as no antithesis at all: just as Wagner did,—and his mastery in this

kind of falseness was of no mean order. To cast side-long
glances at master-morality, at noble morality (—Icelandic
saga is perhaps the greatest documentary evidence of these
values), and at the same time to have the opposite teaching,
the "gospel of the lowly," the doctrine of the need of salvation, on one's lips!... Incidentally, I admire the modesty of
Christians who go to Bayreuth. As for myself, I could not
endure to hear the sound of certain words on Wagner's lips.
There are some concepts which are too good for Bayreuth ...
What? Christianity adjusted for female Wagnerites, perhaps
by female Wagnerites—for, in his latter days Wagner was
thoroughly feminini generis—? Again I say, the Christians of
to-day are too modest for me.... If Wagner were a Christian,
then Liszt was perhaps a Father of the Church!—The need of
salvation, the quintessence of all Christian needs, has nothing in common with such clowns; it is the most straightfor-
ward expression of decadence, it is the most convincing and
most painful affirmation of decadence, in sublime symbols
and practices. The Christian wishes to be rid of himself. Le
moi est toujours haissable. Noble morality, master-morality,
on the other hand, is rooted in a triumphant saying of yea to
one's self,—it is the self-affirmation and self-glorification of
life; it also requires sublime symbols and practices; but only
"because its heart is too full." The whole of beautiful art and
of great art belongs here; their common essence is gratitude.
But we must allow it a certain instinctive repugnance to
décadents, and a scorn and horror of the latter's symbolism:
such things almost prove it. The noble Romans considered
Christianity as a fœda superstitio: let me call to your minds
the feelings which the last German of noble taste—Goethe—
had in regard to the cross. It is idle to look for more valuable,
more necessary contrasts.[14]

But the kind of falsity which is characteristic of the Bayreu-
thians is not exceptional to-day. We all know the hybrid concept of the Christian gentleman. This innocence in contradiction, this "clean conscience" in falsehood, is rather modern
par excellence, with it modernity is almost defined. Biologi-
cally, modern man represents a contradiction of values, he

sits between two stools, he says yea and nay in one breath. No wonder that it is precisely in our age that falseness itself became flesh and blood, and even genius! No wonder Wagner dwelt amongst us! It was not without reason that I called Wagner the Cagliostro of modernity.... But all of us, though we do not know it, involuntarily have values, words, formulæ, and morals in our bodies, which are quite antagonistic in their origin—regarded from a physiological standpoint, we are false.... How would a diagnosis of the modern soul begin? With a determined incision into this agglomeration of contradictory instincts, with the total suppression of its antagonistic values, with vivisection applied to its most instructive case. To philosophers the "Case of Wagner" is a windfall—this essay, as you observe, was inspired by gratitude.

Nietzsche Contra Wagner
THE BRIEF OF A PSYCHOLOGIST

Preface

The following chapters have been selected from past works of mine, and not without care. Some of them date back as far as 1877 Here and there, of course, they will be found to have been made a little more intelligible, but above all, more brief. Read consecutively, they can leave no one in any doubt, either concerning myself, or concerning Wagner: we are antipodes. The reader will come to other conclusions, too, in his perusal of these pages: for instance, that this is an essay for psychologists and not for Germans.... I have my readers everywhere, in Vienna, St Petersburg, Copenhagen, Stockholm, Paris, and New York—but I have none in Europe's Flat-land—Germany.... And I might even have something to say to Italians whom I love just as much as I ... Quousque tandem, Crispi ... Triple alliance: a people can only conclude a mésalliance with the "Empire."...

Friedrich Nietzsche.

Turin, Christmas 1888

Wherein I Admire Wagner

I believe that artists very often do not know what they are best able to do. They are much too vain. Their minds are directed to something prouder than merely to appear like little plants, which, with freshness, rareness, and beauty, know how to sprout from their soil with real perfection. The ultimate goodness of their own garden and vineyard is superciliously under-estimated by them, and their love and their insight are not of the same quality. Here is a musician who is a greater master than anyone else in the discovering of tones, peculiar to suffering, oppressed, and tormented souls, who can endow even dumb misery with speech. Nobody can approach him in the colours of late autumn, in the indescribably touching joy of a last, a very last, and all too short gladness; he knows of a chord which expresses those secret and weird midnight hours of the soul, when cause and effect seem to have fallen asunder, and at every moment something may spring out of nonentity. He is happiest of all when creating from out the nethermost depths of human happiness, and, so to speak, from out man's empty bumper, in which the bitterest and most repulsive drops have mingled with the sweetest for good or evil at last. He knows that weary shuffling along of the soul which is no longer able either to spring or to fly, nay, which is no longer able to walk, he has the modest glance of concealed suffering, of understanding without comfort, of leave-taking without word or sign; verily as the Orpheus of all secret misery he is greater than anyone, and many a thing was introduced into art for the first time by him, which hitherto had not been given expression, had not even been thought worthy of art—the cynical revolts, for instance, of which only the greatest sufferer is capable, also many a small and quite microscopical feature of the soul, as it were the scales of its amphibious nature—yes indeed, he is the master of everything very small. But this he refuses to be! His tastes are much more in love with vast walls and with daring frescoes!... He does not see that his spirit has another desire and bent—a totally different outlook—that it prefers to squat peacefully in the corners of broken-down houses: concealed in this way, and hidden even from himself, he paints his really great masterpieces, all of which are very short, often only one bar in length—there, only, does he become quite good, great and perfect, perhaps there alone.— Wagner is one who has suffered much—and this elevates him above other musicians.—I admire Wagner wherever he sets himself to music—

Wherein I Raise Objections

With all this I do not wish to imply that I regard this music as healthy, and least of all in those places where it speaks of

Wagner himself. My objections to Wagner's music are physiological objections. Why should I therefore begin by clothing
them in æsthetic formulæ? Æsthetic is indeed nothing more
than applied physiology—The fact I bring forward, my "petit
fait vrai," is that I can no longer breathe with ease when this
music begins to have its effect upon me; that my foot immediately begins to feel indignant at it and rebels: for what
it needs is time, dance, march; even the young German Kaiser could not march to Wagner's Imperial March,—what my
foot demands in the first place from music is that ecstasy
which lies in good walking, stepping and dancing. But do
not my stomach, my heart, my circulation also protest? Are
not my intestines also troubled? And do I not become hoarse
unawares? ... in order to listen to Wagner I require Gérau-
del's Pastilles.... And then I ask myself, what is it that my
whole body must have from music in general? for there is no
such thing as a soul.... I believe it must have relief: as if all
animal functions were accelerated by means of light, bold,
unfettered, self-reliant rhythms, as if brazen and leaden life
could lose its weight by means of delicate and smooth melodies. My melancholy would fain rest its head in the haunts
and abysses of perfection; for this reason I need music. But
Wagner makes one ill—What do I care about the theatre?
What do I care about the spasms of its moral ecstasies in
which the mob—and who is not the mob to-day?—rejoices?
What do I care about the whole pantomimic hocus-pocus
of the actor? You are beginning to see that I am essentially
anti-theatrical at heart. For the stage, this mob art par excellence, my soul has that deepest scorn felt by every artist
to-day. With a stage success a man sinks to such an extent
in my esteem as to drop out of sight; failure in this quarter
makes me prick my ears, makes me begin to pay attention.
But this was not so with Wagner, next to the Wagner who
created the most unique music that has ever existed there
was the Wagner who was essentially a man of the stage, an
actor, the most enthusiastic mimomaniac that has perhaps
existed on earth, even as a musician. And let it be said en
passant that if Wagner's theory was "drama is the object,

music is only a means"—his practice was from beginning to end "the attitude is the end, drama and even music can never be anything else than means." Music as the manner of accentuating, of strengthening, and deepening dramatic poses and all things which please the senses of the actor; and Wagnerian drama only an opportunity for a host of interesting attitudes!—Alongside of all other instincts he had the dictatorial instinct of a great actor in everything and, as I have already said, as a musician also.—On one occasion, and not without trouble, I made this clear to a Wagnerite pur sang,—clearness and a Wagnerite! I won't say another word. There were reasons for adding; "For heaven's sake, be a little more true unto yourself! We are not in Bayreuth now. In Bayreuth people are only upright in the mass; the individual lies, he even lies to himself. One leaves oneself at home when one goes to Bayreuth, one gives up all right to one's own tongue and choice, to one's own taste and even to one's own courage, one knows these things no longer as one is wont to have them and practice them before God and the world and between one's own four walls. In the theatre no one brings the finest senses of his art with him, and least of all the artist who works for the theatre,—for here loneliness is lacking; everything perfect does not suffer a witness.... In the theatre one becomes mob, herd, woman, Pharisee, electing cattle, patron, idiot—Wagnerite: there, the most personal conscience is bound to submit to the leveling charm of the great multitude, there the neighbour rules, there one becomes a neighbour."

Wagner As A Danger

1

The aim after which more modern music is striving, which is now given the strong but obscure name of "unending melody," can be clearly understood by comparing it to one's feelings on entering the sea. Gradually one loses one's footing and one ultimately abandons oneself to the mercy or fury of the elements: one has to swim. In the solemn, or fiery, swinging movement, first slow and then quick, of old music—one had to do something quite different; one had to dance. The measure which was required for this and the control of certain balanced degrees of time and energy, forced the soul of the listener to continual sobriety of thought.—Upon the counterplay of the cooler currents of air which came from this sobriety, and from the warmer breath of enthusiasm, the charm of all good music rested—Richard Wagner wanted another kind of movement,—he overthrew the physiological first principle of all music before his time. It was no longer a matter of walking or dancing,—we must swim, we must hover.... This perhaps decides the whole matter. "Unending melody" really wants to break all the symmetry of time and strength; it actually scorns these things—Its wealth of invention resides precisely in what to an older ear sounds like rhythmic paradox and abuse. From the imitation or the prevalence of such a taste there would arise a danger for music—so great that we can imagine none greater—the complete degeneration of the feeling for rhythm, chaos in the place of rhythm.... The danger reaches its climax when such music cleaves ever more closely to naturalistic play-acting and pantomime, which governed by no laws of form, aim at effect and nothing more.... Expressiveness at all costs and music a servant, a slave to attitudes—this is the end....

2

What? would it really be the first virtue of a performance (as performing musical artists now seem to believe), under all circumstances to attain to a haut-relief which cannot be surpassed? If this were applied to Mozart, for instance, would it not be a real sin against Mozart's spirit,—Mozart's cheerful, enthusiastic, delightful and loving spirit? He who fortunately was no German, and whose seriousness is a charming and golden seriousness and not by any means that of a German clodhopper.... Not to speak of the earnestness of the "marble statue".... But you seem to think that all music is the music of the "marble statue"?—that all music should, so to speak, spring out of the wall and shake the listener to his very bowels?... Only thus could music have any effect! But on whom would the effect be made? Upon something on which a noble artist ought never to deign to act,—upon the mob, upon the immature! upon the blasés! upon the diseased! upon idiots! upon Wagnerites!...

A Music Without A Future

Of all the arts which succeed in growing on the soil of a particular culture, music is the last plant to appear; maybe because it is the one most dependent upon our innermost feelings, and therefore the last to come to the surface—at a time when the culture to which it belongs is in its autumn season and beginning to fade. It was only in the art of the Dutch masters that the spirit of mediæval Christianity found its expression—, its architecture of sound is the youngest, but genuine and legitimate, sister of the Gothic. It was only in Handel's music that the best in Luther and in those like him found its voice, the Judeo-heroic trait which gave the Reformation a touch of greatness-the Old Testament, not the New, become music. It was left to Mozart, to pour out the epoch of Louis XIV., and of the art of Racine and Claude Lorrain, in ringing gold; only in Beethoven's and Rossini's music did the Eighteenth Century sing itself out—the century of enthusiasm, broken ideals, and fleeting joy. All real and original music is a swan song—Even our last form of music, despite its prevalence and its will to prevail, has perhaps only a short time to live, for it sprouted from a soil which was in the throes of a rapid subsidence,—of a culture which will soon be submerged. A certain catholicism of feeling, and a predilection for some ancient indigenous (so-called national) ideals and eccentricities, was its first condition. Wagner's appropriation of old sagas and songs, in which scholarly prejudice taught us to see something German par excellence—now we laugh at it all, the resurrection of these Scandinavian monsters with a thirst for ecstatic sensuality and spiritualisation—the whole of this taking and giving on Wagner's part, in the matter of subjects, characters, passions, and nerves, would also give unmistakable expression to the spirit of his music provided that this music, like any other, did not know how to speak about itself save ambiguously: for musica is a woman.... We must not let ourselves be misled concerning this state of things, by the fact that at this very moment we are living in a reaction, in the heart itself of a reaction. The age of international wars, of ultramontane martyrdom, in fact, the whole interlude-character which typifies the present condition of Europe, may indeed help an art like Wagner's to sudden glory, without, however, in the least ensuring its future prosperity. The Germans themselves have no future....

We Antipodes

Perhaps a few people, or at least my friends, will remember that I made my first plunge into life armed with some errors and some exaggerations, but that, in any case, I began with hope in my heart. In the philosophical pessimism of the nineteenth century, I recognized—who knows by what by-paths of personal experience—the symptom of a higher power of thought, a more triumphant plenitude of life, than had manifested itself hitherto in the philosophies of Hume, Kant and Hegel!—I regarded tragic knowledge as the most beautiful luxury of our culture, as its most precious, most noble, most dangerous kind of prodigality; but, nevertheless, in view of its overflowing wealth, as a justifiable luxury. In the same way, I began by interpreting Wagner's music as the expression of a Dionysian powerfulness of soul. In it I thought I heard the earthquake by means of which a primeval life-force, which had been constrained for ages, was seeking at last to burst its bonds, quite indifferent to how much of that which nowadays calls itself culture, would thereby be shaken to ruins. You see how I misinterpreted, you see also, what I bestowed upon Wagner and Schopenhauer—myself.... Every art and every philosophy may be regarded either as a cure or as a stimulant to ascending or declining life: they always presuppose suffering and sufferers. But there are two kinds of sufferers:—those that suffer from overflowing vitality, who need Dionysian art and require a tragic insight into, and a tragic outlook upon, the phenomenon life,—and there are those who suffer from reduced vitality, and who crave for repose, quietness, calm seas, or else the intoxication, the spasm, the bewilderment which art and philosophy provide. Revenge upon life itself—this is the most voluptuous form of intoxication for such indigent souls!... Now Wagner responds quite as well as Schopenhauer to the twofold cravings of these people,—they both deny life, they both slander it but precisely on this account they are my antipodes.—The richest creature, brimming over with vitality,—the Dionysian God and man, may not only allow himself to gaze upon the horrible and the questionable; but he can also lend his hand to the terrible deed, and can indulge in all the luxury of destruction, disaggregation, and negation,—in him evil, purposelessness and ugliness, seem just as allowable as they are in nature—because of his bursting plenitude of creative and rejuvenating powers, which are able to convert every desert into a luxurious land of plenty. Conversely, it is the greatest sufferer and pauper in vitality, who is most in need of mildness, peace and goodness—that which to-day is called humaneness—in thought as well as in action, and possibly of a God whose speciality is to be a God of the sick, a Saviour, and also of logic or the abstract intelligibility of existence even for idiots (—the typical "free-spirits," like the idealists, and "beautiful souls," are décadents—); in short, of a warm, danger-tight, and narrow confinement, between optimistic horizons which would allow of stultification.... And thus very gradually, I began to understand Epicurus, the opposite of a Dionysian Greek, and also the Christian who in fact is only a kind of Epicurean, and who, with his belief that "faith saves," carries the principle of Hedonism as far as possible—far beyond all intellectual honesty.... If I am ahead of all other psychologists in anything, it is in this fact that my eyes are more keen for tracing those most difficult and most captious of all deductions, in which the largest number of mistakes have been made,—the deduction which makes one infer something concerning the author from his work, something concerning the doer from his deed, something concerning the idealist from the need which produced this ideal, and something concerning the imperious craving which stands at the back of all thinking and valuing—In regard to all artists of what kind soever, I shall now avail myself of this radical distinction: does the creative power in this case arise from a loathing of life, or from an excessive plenitude of life? In Goethe, for instance, an overflow of vitality was creative, in Flaubert—hate: Flaubert, a new edition of Pascal, but as an artist with this instinctive belief at heart: "Flaubert est toujours haissable, l'homme n'est rien, l'œuvre est tout".... He tortured himself when he wrote, just as Pascal tortured himself when he thought—the feelings of both were inclined to be "non-egoistic." ... "Disinterestedness"—principle of decadence, the will to nonentity in art as well as in morality.

Where Wagner Is At Home

Even at the present day, France is still the refuge of the most intellectual and refined culture in Europe, it remains the high school of taste: but one must know where to find this France of taste. The North-German Gazette, for instance, or whoever expresses his sentiments in that paper, thinks that the French are "barbarians,"—as for me, if I had to find the blackest spot on earth, where slaves still required to be liberated, I should turn in the direction of Northern Germany.... But those who form part of that select France take very good care to conceal themselves; they are a small body of men, and there may be some among them who do not stand on very firm legs—a few may be fatalists, hypochondriacs, invalids; others may be enervated, and artificial,—such are those who would fain be artistic,—but all the loftiness and delicacy which still remains to this world, is in their possession. In this France of intellect, which is also the France of pessimism, Schopenhauer is already much more at home than he ever was in Germany, his principal work has already been translated twice, and the second time so excellently that now I prefer to read Schopenhauer in French (—he was an accident among Germans, just as I am—the Germans have no fingers wherewith to grasp us; they haven't any fingers at all,—but only claws). And I do not mention Heine—l'adorable

Heine, as they say in Paris—who long since has passed into the flesh and blood of the more profound and more soulful of French lyricists. How could the horned cattle of Germany know how to deal with the délicatesses of such a nature!—And as to Richard Wagner, it is obvious, it is even glaringly obvious, that Paris is the very soil for him, the more French music adapts itself to the needs of l'âme moderne, the more Wagnerian it will become,—it is far enough advanced in this direction already.—In this respect one should not allow one's self to be misled by Wagner himself—it was simply disgraceful on Wagner's part to scoff at Paris, as he did, in its agony in 1871... In spite of it all, in Germany Wagner is only a misapprehension.—who could be more incapable of understanding anything about Wagner than the Kaiser, for instance?—To everybody familiar with the movement of European culture, this fact, however, is certain, that French romanticism and Richard Wagner are most intimately related. All dominated by literature, up to their very eyes and ears—the first European artists with a universal literary culture,—most of them writers, poets, mediators and minglers of the senses and the arts, all fanatics in expression, great discoverers in the realm of the sublime as also of the ugly and the gruesome, and still greater discoverers in passion, in working for effect, in the art of dressing their windows,—all possessing talent far above their genius,—virtuosos to their backbone, knowing of secret passages to all that seduces, lures, strange and the monstrous, and all opiates for the senses and the understanding. On the whole, a daring dare-devil, magnificently violent, soaring and high-springing crew of artists, who first had to teach their own century—it is the century of the mob—what the concept "artist" meant. But they were ill....

Wagner As The Apostle Of Chastity

1

Is this the German way?
Comes this low bleating forth from German hearts?
Should Teutons, sin repenting, lash themselves,

Or spread their palms with priestly unctuousness,
Exalt their feelings with the censer's fumes,
And cower and quake and bend the trembling knee,
And with a sickly sweetness plead a prayer?
Then ogle nuns, and ring the Ave-bell,
And thus with morbid fervour out-do heaven?
Is this the German way?
Beware, yet are you free, yet your own Lords.
What yonder lures is Rome, Rome's faith sung without
words.

2

There is no necessary contrast between sensuality and
chastity, every good marriage, every genuine love affair is
above this contrast; but in those cases where the contrast
exists, it is very far from being necessarily a tragic one. This,
at least, ought to hold good of all well-constituted and good-
spirited mortals, who are not in the least inclined to reckon
their unstable equilibrium between angel and petite bête,
without further ado, among the objections to existence, the
more refined and more intelligent like Hafis and Goethe,
even regarded it as an additional attraction. It is precisely
contradictions of this kind which lure us to life.... On the
other hand, it must be obvious, that when Circe's unfortunate animals are induced to worship chastity, all they see
and worship therein, is their opposite—oh! and with what
tragic groaning and fervour, may well be imagined—that
same painful and thoroughly superfluous opposition which,
towards the end of his life, Richard Wagner undoubtedly
wished to set to music and to put on the stage, And to what
purpose? we may reasonably ask.

3

And yet this other question can certainly not be circumvented: what business had he actually with that manly (alas!
so unmanly) "bucolic simplicity," that poor devil and son of
nature—Parsifal, whom he ultimately makes a catholic by
such insidious means—what?—was Wagner in earnest with

Parsifal? For, that he was laughed at, I cannot deny, any more than Gottfried Keller can.... We should like to believe that "Parsifal" was meant as a piece of idle gaiety, as the closing act and satyric drama, with which Wagner the tragedian wished to take leave of us, of himself, and above all of tragedy, in a way which befitted him and his dignity, that is to say, with an extravagant, lofty and most malicious parody of tragedy itself, of all the past and terrible earnestness and sorrow of this world, of the most ridiculous form of the unnaturalness of the ascetic ideal, at last overcome. For Parsifal is the subject par excellence for a comic opera.... Is Wagner's "Parsifal" his secret laugh of superiority at himself, the triumph of his last and most exalted state of artistic freedom, of artistic transcendence—is it Wagner able to laugh at himself? Once again we only wish it were so; for what could Parsifal be if he were meant seriously? Is it necessary in his case to say (as I have heard people say) that "Parsifal" is "the product of the mad hatred of knowledge, intellect, and sensuality?" a curse upon the senses and the mind in one breath and in one fit of hatred? an act of apostasy and a return to Christianly sick and obscurantist ideals? And finally even a denial of self, a deletion of self, on the part of an artist who theretofore had worked with all the power of his will in favour of the opposite cause, the spiritualization and sensualization of his art? And not only of his art, but also of his life? Let us remember how enthusiastically Wagner at one time walked in the footsteps of the philosopher Feuerbach. Feuerbach's words "healthy sensuality" struck Wagner in the thirties and forties very much as they struck many other Germans—they called themselves the young Germans—that is to say, as words of salvation. Did he ultimately change his mind on this point? It would seem that he had at least had the desire of changing his doctrine towards the end.... Had the hatred of life become dominant in him as in Flaubert? For "Parsifal" is a work of rancour, of revenge, of the most secret concoction of poisons with which to make an end of the first conditions of life, it is a bad work. The preaching of chastity remains an incitement to unnaturalness: I despise anybody who does not regard "Parsifal" as an outrage upon morality.—

How I Got Rid Of Wagner

1

Already in the summer of 1876, when the first festival at Bayreuth was at its height, I took leave of Wagner in my soul. I cannot endure anything double-faced. Since Wagner had returned to Germany, he had condescended step by step to everything that I despise—even to anti-Semitism.... As a matter of fact, it was then high time to bid him farewell: but the proof of this came only too soon. Richard Wagner, ostensibly the most triumphant creature alive; as a matter of fact, though, a cranky and desperate décadent, suddenly fell helpless and broken on his knees before the Christian cross.... Was there no German at that time who had the eyes to see, and the sympathy in his soul to feel, the ghastly nature of this spectacle? Was I the only one who suffered from it?—Enough, the unexpected event, like a flash of lightning, made me see only too clearly what kind of a place it was that I had just left,—and it also made me shudder as a man shudders who unawares has just escaped a great danger. As I continued my journey alone, I trembled. Not long after this I was ill, more than ill—I was tired;—tired of the continual disappointments over everything which remained for us modern men to be enthusiastic about, of the energy, industry, hope, youth, and love that are squandered everywhere; tired out of loathing for the whole world of idealistic lying and conscience-softening, which, once again, in the case of Wagner, had scored a victory over a man who was of the bravest; and last but not least, tired by the sadness of a ruthless suspicion—that I was now condemned to be ever more and more suspicious, ever more and more contemptuous, ever more and more deeply alone than I had been theretofore. For I had no one save Richard Wagner.... I was always condemned to the society of Germans....

2

Henceforward alone and cruelly distrustful of myself, I then took up sides—not without anger—against myself and for all that which hurt me and fell hard upon me; and thus I found the road to that courageous pessimism which is the opposite of all idealistic falsehood, and which, as it seems to me, is also the road to me—to my mission.... That hidden and dominating thing, for which for long ages we have had no name, until ultimately it comes forth as our mission,—this tyrant in us wreaks a terrible revenge upon us for every attempt we make either to evade him or to escape him, for every one of our experiments in the way of befriending people to whom we do not belong, for every active occupation, however estimable, which may make us diverge from our principal object:— aye, and even for every virtue which would fain protect us from the rigour of our most intimate sense of responsibility. Illness is always the answer, whenever we venture to doubt our right to our mission, whenever we begin to make things too easy for ourselves. Curious and terrible at the same time! It is for our relaxation that we have to pay most dearly! And should we wish after all to return to health, we then have no choice: we are compelled to burden ourselves more heavily than we had been burdened before....

The Psychologist Speaks

1

The oftener a psychologist—a born, an unavoidable psychologist and soul-diviner—turns his attention to the more select cases and individuals, the greater becomes his danger of being suffocated by sympathy: he needs greater hardness and cheerfulness than any other man. For the corruption, the ruination of higher men, is in fact the rule: it is terrible to have such a rule always before our eyes. The manifold torments of the psychologist who has discovered this ruination, who discovers once, and then discovers almost repeatedly throughout all history, this universal inner "hopelessness" of higher men, this eternal "too late!" in every sense—may per-

haps one day be the cause of his "going to the dogs" himself.
In almost every psychologist we may see a tell-tale predilection in favour of intercourse with commonplace and well-
ordered men: and this betrays how constantly he requires
healing, that he needs a sort of flight and forgetfulness, away
from what his insight and incisiveness—from what his "business"—has laid upon his conscience. A horror of his memory is typical of him. He is easily silenced by the judgment
of others, he hears with unmoved countenance how people
honour, admire, love, and glorify, where he has opened his
eyes and seen—or he even conceals his silence by expressly
agreeing with some obvious opinion. Perhaps the paradox
of his situation becomes so dreadful that, precisely where
he has learnt great sympathy, together with great contempt,
the educated have on their part learnt great reverence. And
who knows but in all great instances, just this alone happened: that the multitude worshipped a God, and that the
"God" was only a poor sacrificial animal! Success has always
been the greatest liar—and the "work" itself, the deed, is a
success too; the great statesman, the conqueror, the discov-
erer, are disguised in their creations until they can no longer
be recognized, the "work" of the artist, of the philosopher,
only invents him who has created it, who is reputed to have
created it, the "great men," as they are reverenced, are poor
little fictions composed afterwards; in the world of historical
values counterfeit coinage prevails.

2

Those great poets, for example, such as Byron, Musset,
Poe, Leopardi, Kleist, Gogol (I do not dare to mention much
greater names, but I imply them), as they now appear, and
were perhaps obliged to be: men of the moment, sensuous,
absurd, versatile, light-minded and quick to trust and to
distrust, with souls in which usually some flaw has to be
concealed, often taking revenge with their works for an in-
ternal blemish, often seeking forgetfulness in their soaring
from a too accurate memory, idealists out of proximity to
the mud:—what a torment these great artists are and the

so-called higher men in general, to him who has once found them out! We are all special pleaders in the cause of mediocrity. It is conceivable that it is just from woman—who is clairvoyant in the world of suffering, and, alas! also unfortunately eager to help and save to an extent far beyond her powers—that they have learnt so readily those outbreaks of boundless sympathy which the multitude, above all the reverent multitude, overwhelms with prying and self-gratifying interpretations. This sympathising invariably deceives itself as to its power; woman would like to believe that love can do everything—it is the superstition peculiar to her. Alas, he who knows the heart finds out how poor, helpless, pretentious, and blundering even the best and deepest love is—how much more readily it destroys than saves....

3

The intellectual loathing and haughtiness of every man who has suffered deeply—the extent to which a man can suffer, almost determines the order of rank—the chilling uncertainty with which he is thoroughly imbued and coloured, that by virtue of his suffering he knows more than the shrewdest and wisest can ever know, that he has been familiar with, and "at home" in many distant terrible worlds of which "you know nothing!"—this silent intellectual haughtiness, this pride of the elect of knowledge, of the "initiated," of the almost sacrificed, finds all forms of disguise necessary to protect itself from contact with gushing and sympathizing hands, and in general from all that is not its equal in suffering. Profound suffering makes noble; it separates.—One of the most refined forms of disguise is Epicurism, along with a certain ostentatious boldness of taste which takes suffering lightly, and puts itself on the defensive against all that is sorrowful and profound. There are "cheerful men" who make use of good spirits, because they are misunderstood on account of them—they wish to be misunderstood. There are "scientific minds" who make use of science, because it gives a cheerful appearance, and because love of science leads people to conclude that a person is shallow—they wish to mislead to a false conclusion. There are free insolent spirits which would fain conceal and deny that they are at bottom broken, incurable hearts—this is Hamlet's case: and then folly itself can be the mask of an unfortunate and alas! all too dead-certain knowledge.

Epilogue

1

I have often asked myself whether I am not much more deeply indebted to the hardest years of my life than to any others. According to the voice of my innermost nature, everything necessary, seen from above and in the light of a superior economy, is also useful in itself—not only should one bear it, one should love it.... Amor fati: this is the very core of my being—And as to my prolonged illness, do I not owe much more to it than I owe to my health? To it I owe a higher kind of health, a sort of health which grows stronger under everything that does not actually kill it!—To it, I owe even my philosophy.... Only great suffering is the ultimate emancipator of spirit, for it teaches one that vast suspiciousness which makes an X out of every U, a genuine and proper X, i.e., the antepenultimate letter. Only great suffering; that great suffering, under which we seem to be over a fire of greenwood, the suffering that takes its time—forces us philosophers to descend into our nethermost depths, and to let go of all trustfulness, all good-nature, all whittling-down, all mildness, all mediocrity,—on which things we had formerly staked our humanity. I doubt whether such suffering improves a man; but I know that it makes him deeper.... Supposing we learn to set our pride, our scorn, our strength of will against it, and thus resemble the Indian who, however cruelly he may be tortured, considers himself revenged on his tormentor by the bitterness of his own tongue. Supposing we withdraw from pain into nonentity, into the deaf, dumb, and rigid sphere of self-surrender, self-forgetfulness, self-effacement: one is another person when one leaves these protracted and dangerous exercises in the art of self-mastery, one has one note of interrogation the more, and above all one has the will henceforward to ask more, deeper, sterner, harder, more wicked, and more silent questions, than anyone has ever asked on earth before.... Trust in life has vanished; life itself has become a problem.—But let no one think that one has therefore become a spirit of gloom or a blind owl! Even love of life is still possible,—but it is a different kind of love.... It is the love for a woman whom we doubt....

2

The rarest of all things is this: to have after all another taste—a second taste. Out of such abysses, out of the abyss of great suspicion as well, a man returns as though born again, he has a new skin, he is more susceptible, more full of wickedness; he has a finer taste for joyfulness; he has a more sensitive tongue for all good things; his senses are more cheerful; he has acquired a second, more dangerous, innocence in gladness; he is more childish too, and a hundred times more cunning than ever he had been before.

Oh, how much more repulsive pleasure now is to him, that coarse, heavy, buff-coloured pleasure, which is understood by our pleasure-seekers, our "cultured people," our wealthy folk and our rulers! With how much more irony we now listen to the hubbub as of a country fair, with which the "cultured" man and the man about town allow themselves to be forced through art, literature, music, and with the help of intoxicating liquor, to "intellectual enjoyments." How the stage-cry of passion now stings our ears; how strange to our taste the whole romantic riot and sensuous bustle, which the cultured mob are so fond of, together with its aspirations to the sublime, to the exalted and the distorted, have become. No: if we convalescents require an art at all, it is another art—-a mocking, nimble, volatile, divinely undisturbed, divinely artificial art, which blazes up like pure flame into a cloudless sky! But above all, an art for artists, only for artists! We are, after all, more conversant with that which is in the highest degree necessary—cheerfulness, every kind of cheerfulness, my friends!... We men of knowledge, now know something only too well: oh how well we have learnt by this time, to forget, not to know, as artists!... As to our future: we shall scarcely be found on the track of those Egyptian youths who break into temples at night, who embrace statues, and would fain unveil, strip, and set in broad daylight, everything which there are excellent reasons to keep concealed.[15] No, we are disgusted with this bad taste, this will to truth, this search after truth "at all costs;" this madness of adolescence, "the love of truth;" we are now too experienced, too serious, too joyful, too scorched, too profound for that.... We no longer believe that truth remains truth when it is unveiled,—we have lived enough to understand this.... To-day it seems to us good form not to strip everything naked, not to be present at all things, not to desire to "know" all. "Tout comprendre c'est tout mépriser."... "Is it true," a little girl once asked her mother, "that the beloved Father is everywhere?—I think it quite improper,"—a hint to philosophers.... The shame with which Nature has concealed herself behind riddles and enigmas should be held in higher esteem. Perhaps truth is a woman who has reasons for not revealing her reasons?... Perhaps her name, to use a Greek word is Baubo?—Oh these Greeks, they understood the art of living! For this it is needful to halt bravely at the surface, at the fold, at the skin, to worship appearance, and to believe in forms, tones, words, and the whole Olympus of appearance! These Greeks were superficial—from profundity.... And are we not returning to precisely the same thing, we dare-devils of intellect who have scaled the highest and most dangerous pinnacles of present thought, in order to look around us from that height, in order to look down from that height? Are we not precisely in this respect—Greeks? Worshippers of form, of tones, of words? Precisely on that account—artists?

Selected Aphorisms from Nietzsche's Retrospect of his Years of Friendship with Wagner

(Summer 1878)

1

My blunder was this, I travelled to Bayreuth with an ideal in my breast, and was thus doomed to experience the bitterest disappointment. The preponderance of ugliness, grotesqueness and strong pepper thoroughly repelled me.

2

I utterly disagree with those who were dissatisfied with the decorations, the scenery and the mechanical contrivances at Bayreuth. Far too much industry and ingenuity was applied to the task of chaining the imagination to matters which did not belie their epic origin. But as to the naturalism of the attitudes, of the singing, compared with the orchestra!! What affected, artificial and depraved tones, what a distortion of nature, were we made to hear!

3

We are witnessing the death agony of the last Art: Bayreuth has convinced me of this.

4

My picture of Wagner, completely surpassed him; I had depicted an ideal monster—one, however, which is perhaps quite capable of kindling the enthusiasm of artists. The real Wagner, Bayreuth as it actually is, was only like a bad, final proof, pulled on inferior paper from the engraving which was my creation. My longing to see real men and their motives, received an extraordinary impetus from this humiliating experience.

5

This, to my sorrow, is what I realized; a good deal even struck me with sudden fear. At last I felt, however, that if only I could be strong enough to take sides against myself and what I most loved I would find the road to truth and get solace and encouragement from it—and in this way I became filled with a sensation of joy far greater than that upon which I was now voluntarily turning my back.

6

I was in love with art, passionately in love, and in the whole of existence saw nothing else than art—and this at an age when, reasonably enough, quite different passions usually possess the soul.

7

Goethe said: "The yearning spirit within me, which in earlier years I may perhaps have fostered too earnestly, and which as I grew older I tried my utmost to combat, did not seem becoming in the man, and I therefore had to strive to attain to more complete freedom." Conclusion?—I have had to do the same.

8

He who wakes us always wounds us.

9

I do not possess the talent of being loyal, and what is still worse, I have not even the vanity to try to appear as if I did.

10

He who accomplishes anything that lies beyond the vision and the experience of his acquaintances,—provokes envy and hatred masked as pity,—prejudice regards the work as decadence, disease, seduction. Long faces.

11

I frankly confess that I had hoped that by means of art the Germans would become thoroughly disgusted with decaying Christianity—I regarded German mythology as a solvent, as a means of accustoming people to polytheism.

What a fright I had over the Catholic revival!!

12

It is possible neither to suffer sufficiently acutely from life, nor to be so lifeless and emotionally weak, as to have need of Wagner's art, as to require it as a medium. This is the principal reason of one's opposition to it, and not baser motives; something to which we are not driven by any personal need, and which we do not require, we cannot esteem so highly.

13

It is a question either of no longer requiring Wagner's art, or of still requiring it.

Gigantic forces lie concealed in it: it drives one beyond its own domain.

14

Goethe said: "Are not Byron's audacity, sprightliness and grandeur all creative? We must beware of always looking for this quality in that which is perfectly pure and moral. All greatness is creative the moment we realize it." This should be applied to Wagner's art.

15

We shall always have to credit Wagner with the fact that in the second half of the nineteenth century he impressed art upon our memory as an important and magnificent thing. True, he did this in his own fashion, and this was not the fashion of upright and far-seeing men.

16

Wagner versus the cautious, the cold and the contented of the world—in this lies his greatness—he is a stranger to his age—he combats the frivolous and the super-smart—But he also fights the just, the moderate, those who delight in the world (like Goethe), and the mild, the people of charm, the scientific among men—this is the reverse of the medal.

17

Our youth was up in arms against the soberness of the age. It plunged into the cult of excess, of passion, of ecstasy, and of the blackest and most austere conception of the world.

18

Wagner pursues one form of madness, the age another form. Both carry on their chase at the same speed, each is as blind and as unjust as the other.

19

It is very difficult to trace the course of Wagner's inner development—no trust must be placed in his own description of his soul's experiences. He writes party-pamphlets for his followers.

20

It is extremely doubtful whether Wagner is able to bear witness about himself.

21

There are men who try in vain to make a principle out of themselves. This was the case with Wagner.

22

Wagner's obscurity concerning final aims; his non-antique fogginess.

23

All Wagner's ideas straightway become manias; he is tyrannized over by them. How can such a man allow himself to be tyrannized over in this way! For instance by his hatred of Jews. He kills his themes like his "ideas," by means of his violent love of repeating them. The problem of excessive length and breadth; he bores us with his raptures.

24

"C'est la rage de voulour penser et sentir au delà de sa force" (Doudan). The Wagnerites.

25

Wagner whose ambition far exceeds his natural gifts, has tried an incalculable number of times to achieve what lay beyond his powers—but it almost makes one shudder to see someone assail with such persistence that which defies conquest—the fate of his constitution.

26

He is always thinking of the most extreme expression,—in every word. But in the end superlatives begin to pall.

27

There is something which is in the highest degree suspicious in Wagner, and that is Wagner's suspicion. It is such a strong trait in him, that on two occasions I doubted whether he were a musician at all.

28

The proposition: "in the face of perfection there is no salvation save love,"[16] is thoroughly Wagnerian. Profound jealousy of everything great from which he can draw fresh ideas. Hatred of all that which he cannot approach, the Renaissance, French and Greek art in style.

29

Wagner is jealous of all periods that have shown restraint: he despises beauty and grace, and finds only his own virtues in the "Germans," and even attributes all his failings to them.

30

Wagner has not the power to unlock and liberate the soul of those he frequents. Wagner is not sure of himself, but distrustful and arrogant. His art has this effect upon artists, it is envious of all rivals.

31

Plato's Envy. He would fain monopolize Socrates. He saturates the latter with himself, pretends to adorn him (καλὸς Σωκράτης), and tries to separate all Socratists from him in order himself to appear as the only true apostle. But his historical presentation of him is false, even to a parlous degree: just as Wagner's presentation of Beethoven and Shakespeare is false.

32

When a dramatist speaks about himself he plays a part: this is inevitable. When Wagner speaks about Bach and Beethoven he speaks like one for whom he would fain be taken. But he impresses only those who are already convinced, for his dissimulation and his genuine nature are far too violently at variance.

33

Wagner struggles against the "frivolity" in his nature, which to him the ignoble (as opposed to Goethe) constituted the joy of life.

34

Wagner has the mind of the ordinary man who prefers to trace things to one cause. The Jews do the same: one aim, therefore one Saviour. In this way he simplifies German and culture; wrongly but strongly.

35

Wagner admitted all this to himself often enough when in private communion with his soul. I only wish he had also admitted it publicly. For what constitutes the greatness of a character if it is not this, that he who possesses it is able to take sides even against himself in favour of truth.

Wagner's Teutonism

36

That which is un-German in Wagner. He lacks the German charm and grace of a Beethoven, a Mozart, a Weber; he also lacks the flowing, cheerful fire (Allegro con brio) of Beethoven and Weber. He cannot be free and easy without being grotesque. He lacks modesty, indulges in big drums, and always tends to surcharge his effect. He is not the good official that Bach was. Neither has he that Goethean calm in regard to his rivals.

37

Wagner always reaches the high-water mark of his vanity when he speaks of the German nature (incidentally it is also the height of his imprudence); for, if Frederick the Great's justice, Goethe's nobility and freedom from envy, Beethoven's sublime resignation, Bach's delicately transfigured spiritual life,—if steady work performed without any thought of glory and success, and without envy, constitute the true German qualities, would it not seem as if Wagner almost wished to prove he is no German?

38

Terrible wildness, abject sorrow, emptiness, the shudder of joy, unexpectedness,—in short all the qualities peculiar to the Semitic race! I believe that the Jews approach Wagner's art with more understanding than the Aryans do.

39

A passage concerning the Jews, taken from Taine.—As it happens, I have misled the reader, the passage does not concern Wagner at all.—But can it be possible that Wagner is a Jew? In that case we could readily understand his dislike of

Jews.[17]

40

Wagner's art is absolutely the art of the age: an æsthetic age would have rejected it. The more subtle people amongst us actually do reject it even now. The coarsifying of everything æsthetic.—Compared with Goethe's ideal it is very far behind. The moral contrast of these self-indulgent burningly loyal creatures of Wagner, acts like a spur, like an irritant and even this sensation is turned to account in obtaining an effect.

41

What is it in our age that Wagner's art expresses? That brutality and most delicate weakness which exist side by side, that running wild of natural instincts, and nervous hyper-sensitiveness, that thirst for emotion which arises from fatigue and the love of fatigue.—All this is understood by the Wagnerites.

42

Stupefaction or intoxication constitute all Wagnerian art. On the other hand I could mention instances in which Wagner stands higher, in which real joy flows from him.

43

The reason why the figures in Wagner's art behave so madly, is because he greatly feared lest people would doubt that they were alive.

44

Wagner's art is an appeal to inartistic people; all means are welcomed which help towards obtaining an effect. It is calculated not to produce an artistic effect but an effect upon the nerves in general.

45

Apparently in Wagner we have an art for everybody, because coarse and subtle means seem to be united in it. Albeit its pre-requisite may be musico-æsthetic education, and particularly with moral indifference.

46

In Wagner we find the most ambitious combination of all means with the view of obtaining the strongest effect whereas genuine musicians quietly develop individual genres.

47

Dramatists are borrowers—their principal source of wealth—artistic thoughts drawn from the epos. Wagner borrowed from classical music besides. Dramatists are constructive geniuses, they are not inventive and original as the epic poets are. Drama takes a lower rank than the epos: it presupposes a coarser and more democratic public.

48

Wagner does not altogether trust music. He weaves kindred sensations into it in order to lend it the character of greatness. He measures himself on others; he first of all gives his listeners intoxicating drinks in order to lead them into believing that it was the music that intoxicated them.

49

The same amount of talent and industry which makes the classic, when it appears some time too late, also makes the baroque artist like Wagner.

50

Wagner's art is calculated to appeal to short-sighted people—one has to get much too close up to it (Miniature): it also appeals to long-sighted people, but not to those with normal sight.

Contradictions in the Idea of Musical Drama

51

Just listen to the second act of the "Götterdämmerung," without the drama. It is chaotic music, as wild as a bad dream, and it is as frightfully distinct as if it desired to make itself clear even to deaf people. This volubility with nothing to say is alarming. Compared with it the drama is a genuine relief.—Is the fact that this music when heard alone, is, as a whole intolerable (apart from a few intentionally isolated parts) in its favour? Suffice it to say that this music without its accompanying drama, is a perpetual contradiction of all the highest laws of style belonging to older music: he who thoroughly accustoms himself to it, loses all feeling for these laws. But has the drama been improved thanks to this addition? A symbolic interpretation has been affixed to it, a sort of philological commentary, which sets fetters upon the inner and free understanding of the imagination—it is tyrannical. Music is the language of the commentator, who talks the whole of the time and gives us no breathing space. Moreover his is a difficult language which also requires to be explained. He who step by step has mastered, first the libretto (language!), then converted it into action in his mind's eye, then sought out and understood, and became familiar with the musical symbolism thereto: aye, and has fallen in love with all three things: such a man then experiences a great joy. But how exacting! It is quite impossible to do this save for a few short moments,—such tenfold attention on the part of one's eyes, ears, understanding, and feeling, such acute activity in apprehending without any productive reaction, is far too exhausting!—Only the very fewest behave in this way: how is it then that so many are affected? Because most people are only intermittingly attentive, and are inattentive for sometimes whole passages at a stretch; because they bestow their undivided attention now upon the music, later upon the drama, and anon upon the scenery—that is to say they take the work to pieces.—But in this way the kind of work we are discussing is condemned: not the drama but a moment of it is the result, an arbitrary selection. The creator of a new genre should consider this! The arts should not always be dished up together,—but we should imitate the moderation of the ancients which is truer to human nature.

52

Wagner reminds one of lava which blocks its own course by congealing, and suddenly finds itself checked by dams which it has itself built. There is no Allegro con fuoco for him.

53

I compare Wagner's music, which would fain have the same effect as speech, with that kind of sculptural relief which would have the same effect as painting. The highest laws of style are violated, and that which is most sublime can no longer be achieved.

54

The general heaving, undulating and rolling of Wagner's art.

55

In regard to Wagner's rejection of form, we are reminded of Goethe's remark in conversation with Eckermann: "there is no great art in being brilliant if one respects nothing."

56

Once one theme is over, Wagner is always embarrassed as to how to continue. Hence the long preparation, the suspense. His peculiar craftiness consisted in transvaluing his weakness into virtues.—

57

The lack of melody and the poverty of melody in Wagner. Melody is a whole consisting of many beautiful proportions, it is the reflection of a well-ordered soul. He strives after melody; but if he finds one, he almost suffocates it in his embrace.

58

The natural nobility of a Bach and a Beethoven, the beautiful soul (even of a Mendelssohn) are wanting in Wagner. He is one degree lower.

59

Wagner imitates himself again and again—mannerisms. That is why he was the quickest among musicians to be imitated. It is so easy.

60

Mendelssohn who lacked the power of radically staggering one (incidentally this was the talent of the Jews in the Old Testament), makes up for this by the things which were his own, that is to say: freedom within the law, and noble emotions kept within the limits of beauty.

61

Liszt, the first representative of all musicians, but no musician. He was the prince, not the statesman. The conglomerate of a hundred musicians' souls, but not enough of a personality to cast his own shadow upon them.

62

The most wholesome phenomenon is Brahms, in whose music there is more German blood than in that of Wagner's. With these words I would say something complimentary, but by no means wholly so.

63

In Wagner's writings there is no greatness or peace, but presumption. Why?

64

Wagner's Style.—The habit he acquired, from his earliest days, of having his say in the most important matters without a sufficient knowledge of them, has rendered him the obscure and incomprehensible writer that he is. In addition to this he aspired to imitating the witty newspaper article, and finally acquired that presumption which readily joins hands with carelessness "and, behold, it was very good."

65

I am alarmed at the thought of how much pleasure I could find in Wagner's style, which is so careless as to be unworthy of such an artist.

66

In Wagner, as in Brahms, there is a blind denial of the healthy, in his followers this denial is deliberate and conscious.

67

Wagner's art is for those who are conscious of an essential blunder in the conduct of their lives. They feel either that they have checked a great nature by a base occupation, or squandered it through idle pursuits, a conventional marriage, etc. etc.

In this quarter the condemnation of the world is the outcome of the condemnation of the ego.

68

Wagnerites do not wish to alter themselves in any way, they live discontentedly in insipid, conventional and brutal circumstances—only at intervals does art have to raise them as by magic above these things. Weakness of will.

69

Wagner's art is for scholars who do not dare to become philosophers: they feel discontented with themselves and are generally in a state of obtuse stupefaction—from time to time they take a bath in the opposite conditions.

70

I feel as if I had recovered from an illness: with a feeling of unutterable joy I think of Mozart's Requiem. I can once more enjoy simple fare.

71

I understand Sophocles' development through and through—it was the repugnance to pomp and pageantry.

72

I gained an insight into the injustice of idealism, by noticing that I avenged myself on Wagner for the disappointed hopes I had cherished of him.

73

I leave my loftiest duty to the end, and that is to thank Wagner and Schopenhauer publicly, and to make them as it were take sides against themselves.

74

I counsel everybody not to fight shy of such paths (Wagner and Schopenhauer). The wholly unphilosophic feeling of remorse, has become quite strange to me.

Wagner's Effects

75

We must strive to oppose the false after-effects of Wagner's art. If he, in order to create Parsifal, is forced to pump fresh strength from religious sources, this is not an example but a danger.

76

I entertain the fear that the effects of Wagner's art will ultimately pour into that torrent which takes its rise on the other side of the mountains, and which knows how to flow even over mountains.[18]

Footnotes

[1] It should be noted that the first and second editions of these essays on Wagner appeared in pamphlet form, for which the above first preface was written.

[2] Fisher Unwin, 1911

[3] T. N. Foulis, 1910.

[4] See Richard Wagner, by Houston Stuart Chamberlain (translated by G. A. Hight), pp. 15, 16

[5] Constable & Co., 1911

[6] See Author's Preface to "The Case of Wagner" in this volume.

[7] Senta is the heroine in the "Flying Dutchman"—Tr.

[8] A character in "Tannhauser."—Tr.

[9] See "The Will to Power," vol. ii., authorised English edition.—Tr.

[10] Note.—It was a real disaster for æsthetics when the word drama got to be translated by "action." Wagner is not the only culprit here, the whole world does the same,—even the philologists who ought to know better. What ancient drama had in view was grand pathetic scenes,—it even excluded action (or placed it before the piece or behind the scenes). The word drama is of Doric origin, and according to the usage of the Dorian language it meant "event," "history,"—both words in a hieratic sense. The oldest drama represented local legends, "sacred history," upon which the foundation of the cult rested (—thus it was not "action," but fatality. δρᾶν in Doric has nothing to do with action).

[11] Hegel and his school wrote notoriously obscure German.—Tr.

[12] Was Wagner a German at all? There are reasons enough for putting this question. It is difficult to find a single German trait in his character. Great learner that he was, he naturally imitated a great deal that was German—but that is all. His very soul contradicts everything which hitherto

has been regarded as German, not to mention German musicians!—His father was an actor of the name of Geyer.... That which has been popularized hitherto as "Wagner's life" is fable convenue if not something worse. I confess my doubts on any point which is vouched for by Wagner alone. He was not proud enough to be able to suffer the truth about himself. Nobody had less pride than he. Like Victor Hugo he remained true to himself even in his biography,—he remained an actor.

[13] This undoubtedly refers to Nietzsche's only disciple and friend, Peter Gast—Tr.

[14] My "Genealogy of Morals" contains the best exposition of the antithesis "noble morality" and "Christian morality"; a more decisive turning point in the history of religious and moral science does not perhaps exist. This book, which is a touchstone by which I can discover who are my peers, rejoices in being accessible only to the most elevated and most severe minds: the others have not the ears to hear me. One must have one's passion in things, wherein no one has passion nowadays.

[15] An allusion to Schiller's poem: "Das verschleierte Bild zu Sais."—Tr.

[16] What Schiller said of Goethe.—Tr.

[17] See note on page 44.

[18] It should be noted that the German Catholic party is called the Ultramontane Party. The river which can thus flow over mountains is Catholicism, towards which Nietzsche thought Wagner's art to be tending.—Tr.

CPSIA information can be obtained
at www.ICGtesting.com
Printed in the USA
BVHW080717250719
554326BV00002B/410/P

9 781612 039695